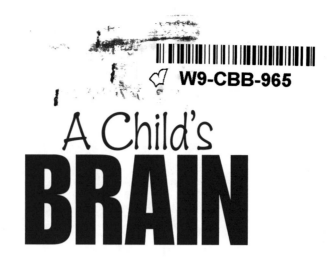

A Child's
BRAIN

A Child's BRAIN

The Need for Nurture

Robert Sylwester

CORWIN
A SAGE Company

Illustrations by Peter Sylwester

For information:

Corwin
A SAGE Company
2455 Teller Road
Thousand Oaks, California 91320
(800) 233-9936
Fax: (800) 417-2466
www.corwin.com

SAGE Ltd.
1 Oliver's Yard
55 City Road
London EC1Y 1SP
United Kingdom

SAGE India Pvt. Ltd.
B 1/I 1 Mohan Cooperative
    Industrial Area
Mathura Road, New Delhi
India 110 044

SAGE Asia-Pacific Pte. Ltd.
33 Pekin Street #02-01
Far East Square
Singapore 048763

Printed in the United States of America.

Library of Congress Cataloging-in-Publication Data

Sylwester, Robert.
A child's brain: the need for nurture/Robert Sylwester.
     p. cm.
"A SAGE Company."
Includes bibliographical references and index.
ISBN 978-1-4129-6271-1 (pbk. : alk. paper)
    1. Cognitive learning. 2. Brain. 3. Effective teaching. 4. Early childhood education.
I. Title.

LB1062.S95 2010
370.15'2—dc22   2010020565

This book is printed on acid-free paper.

10   11   12   13   14   10   9   8   7   6   5   4   3   2   1

Acquisitions Editor:	Carol Chambers Collins
Associate Editor:	Megan Bedell
Editorial Assistant:	Sarah Bartlett
Production Editor:	Cassandra Margaret Seibel
Copy Editor:	Adam Dunham
Typesetter:	C&M Digitals (P) Ltd.
Proofreader:	Christina West
Indexer:	Kathy Paparchontis
Cover Designer:	Karine Hovsepian

Contents

Acknowledgments

Corwin gratefully acknowledges the contributions of the following reviewers:

Barbara Clark, Professor Emeritus
California State University, Los Angeles
Los Angeles, CA

Lynn Kaszynski, Principal
Harrison Street Elementary School
Subury, OH

David A. Sousa, Educational Consultant
Palm Beach, FL

Tracey Tokuhama-Espinosa, Director
Professor of Education
Center for Evaluation and Academic Excellence
Universidad San Francisco de Quito
Quito, Ecuador

Sonia Trehan Kelly, Director
Blue River Montessori School
Duxbury, MA

About the Author

Robert Sylwester is an emeritus professor of education at the University of Oregon who focuses on the educational implications of new developments in science and technology. He has written 20 books and curricular programs and 200-plus journal articles. His most recent books are *The Adolescent Brain: Reaching for Autonomy* (2007) and *How to Explain a Brain: An Educator's Handbook of Brain Terms and Cognitive Processes* (2005). He received two Distinguished Achievement Awards from The Education Press Association of America for his syntheses of cognitive science research, published in *Educational Leadership*. He has made 1600-plus conference and staff-development presentations on educationally significant developments in brain and stress theory and research. He wrote a monthly column for the Internet journal *Brain Connection*, throughout its 2000 to 2009 existence, and is now a regular contributor to the *Information Age Education Newsletter* (http://i-a-e.org/).

Introduction

My teaching career began almost 60 years ago in a one-room rural elementary school. I was clueless, but we all survived the year. I taught there for four stimulating years, and the experience gave me an introduction to the range of childhood and early adolescence development that I couldn't possibly have otherwise experienced.

The school, located within a farm and forest area, had a stream flowing behind it. My avid interest in biology meant that we spent a lot of time outside studying the ecology of the area—probably at the expense of *book learning*. Because we had a bus, and I was the driver, we could also easily go on field trips to other interesting places. We had an enjoyable time, and the students I met in later years had gone on to good lives. I reconnected with a dozen of them recently when I was invited to participate in the community's centennial celebration. I thus have no regrets or apologies for my befuddled professional beginning.

The area is now decidedly suburban—houses, malls, and four-lane streets. Children play in tended parks. State school standards are presumably being assessed in large, well-equipped schools.

World War II had ended five years before I became a teacher, and the United States had embarked on a post-war building boom during which the German Autobahn morphed into the U.S. Interstate Highway System, and various wartime technological advances eventually led to television, computers, and video games.

What we didn't understand at the midpoint of the 20th century was how a brain and much of the rest of biology worked. Childhood infectious diseases were a threat, and most learning disabilities were an enigma. DNA was discovered four years after I completed my degree in biology and wandered into teaching.

Our understanding of teaching and parenting were similarly rudimentary, although folks had been doing both for millennia. We could observe and try to shape the behavior of children with combinations of rewards and punishments, but adults were never sure if the young developed because of—or despite—their efforts.

As I approach the end of my career, I can't help but realize how different the world is for 21st-century parents and teachers who are now beginning the challenges I faced as a father and educator in the middle of the 20th century.

I don't agree with the common tendency to reflect on the past as idyllic and the future as terrifying. What I did then was pleasant enough for me to stay with it, but if I had to begin adult life anew, being a 21st-century parent and teacher would be an even more stimulating and optimistic challenge—and mostly because we know so much more about the underlying biology and neurobiology of childhood and adolescence.

CHILDHOOD IN HUMAN LIFE

We're individuals within a social species, and most of us live in a democratic society. The first 20 years of our life are devoted to mastering the knowledge and skills that are necessary for an effective sense of self, harmonious relationships with family and friends, and effective citizenship within a democratic society. As autonomous productive adults, we then practice what we learned and help yet another generation become competent human beings. This book will thus focus on the knowledge and skills that adults need in order to nurture the next generation—their own children and the children of others.

Although we have the same basic brain throughout our life, it continually adapts itself to new biological and environmental circumstances. Our brain's initial 20-year developmental trajectory moves it from potential to prepared competence levels during two distinct decade-long stages: childhood and adolescence. Our body/brain must be reared within a sheltered nurturing environment during its vulnerability in utero and in childhood, and then during adolescence it must be encouraged to gradually move toward the appropriate and effective autonomous thought and action that is expected of adults.

Adults protect children. They educate them about how the world works, and they make the decisions for them that their immature brains aren't yet equipped to make. Family and school are central to this process.

Adults mentor adolescents. They provide them with opportunities to make the kinds of nonthreatening decisions that will enhance their subsequent ability to make appropriate, more complex adult decisions. Peer relationships become increasingly important to adolescents. Unconditional love and positive role modeling from committed significant adults are very important throughout both developmental decades.

Although children often grouse about adult requests and decisions, they can't survive on their own and so are much more compliant than adolescents—who are reaching for autonomy. Their necessary basic trust in adult judgment thus allows them to observe and learn from appropriate adult behavior, but it also makes them vulnerable to various forms of adult misbehavior that can impair their development. Societies have therefore developed parental back-up systems. Extended family, teachers, social workers, coaches, scouting leaders, religious guides, police, and others combine their efforts to help ensure that children are properly sheltered and nurtured. The ancient aphorism "It takes a village to rear a child" is apt.

The Book's Focus and Organization

This book is a companion to my earlier book, *The Adolescent Brain: Reaching for Autonomy* (2007). It is directed principally to educators and parents, but it is also meant for other adults who work with children. It will combine information about child and cognitive development with general but practical suggestions on how to enhance childhood. Since caregivers confront a myriad of specific nurturing challenges, general guidelines are more useful in a book like this than specific activities that are directed to only some of the readers. Thus, think of any specific suggestions in the book as akin to seasoning in cooking—added *flavor* within the book's principal focus on the nature and role of childhood in human life.

An important corollary audience is the children with whom the adult readers interact. Children are fascinated by their own brain systems and processes, and they need to understand them. We don't have a history of providing children with this kind of information because it has only recently emerged. For example, we teach students how to read but not how and where reading occurs within their brain or why reading is biologically and culturally important. I believe that a functional understanding of the neurobiology of a system or behavior enhances its mastery. The many nontechnical explanations, metaphors, and analogies in the book were thus developed for relatively easy transmission to children, who have a very limited understanding of biology.

Chapters 1 through 4 will focus on the underlying biology of childhood—providing nontechnical explanations of the body/brain systems that develop during pregnancy, infancy, and childhood. As indicated above, parents, educators, and other adults have effectively reared children for millennia with practically no understanding of the neurobiology of childhood, but this fascinating information is now becoming available— and it can enhance the nurturing behavior of informed adults.

Our brain is awesomely complex, but it also has an elegant functional simplicity. It's thus possible for people with a limited understanding of biology (and this includes children) to develop a functional understanding of basic brain systems and processes. As this scientific information is increasingly affecting public policy and practice, it's especially important now that citizens who nurture children understand the underlying biology of childhood.

Chapters 5 through 12 will focus on childhood experiences that can enhance or delay development. These include those that maintain and enhance their body/brain, begin the search toward self that occurs during childhood, and make and maintain personal and technological relationships within and beyond their family. These chapters will draw on the rich existing literature of parenting and teaching that is now incorporating new discoveries in genetics, the cognitive neurosciences, medicine, and other related areas of biology.

The book's Glossary will define technical terms (identified in **bold** the first time they appear in the text), and the Appendices will provide more technical explanations of selected brain systems for those who wish it. The References and Resources section will suggest useful supplementary print and electronic information.

I've explored many of the concepts and themes in this book during my long career as a teacher and writer—and especially during the past decade through my monthly column in the *Brain Connection* website. It's thus been interesting to revisit and update what I had written over the years and to realize how much our understanding of childhood, parenting, and teaching has advanced during my professional career.

My principal mentors in my life have sequentially been my parents, my siblings, my wife Ruth, our seven children—and now our 20 grandchildren, who have given me yet another marvelous perspective of childhood. I was fortunate that my career paralleled such a wonderful time of discovery in the cognitive neurosciences because I could thus learn through personal and print contacts from those who made the discoveries that will profoundly affect how we perceive life and learning. I've further had the opportunity to work with many valued colleagues and editors who helped me to find my professional voice. Thanks to all of you.

Part 1

Understanding Childhood

Nature and Nurture

From Past to Present

Most animals begin life with all or most of their survival systems functional. Their independent life thus begins immediately or shortly after birth. Humans are a notable exception. We're basically helpless at birth and for a long time afterwards. The principal reason is that, because our three-pound adult brain is much larger than our mother's birth canal, we're born with a one-pound basic brain that can traverse the canal, but can't regulate an independent life.

During its initial 20-year post-birth development, our brain adds two pounds of mass and accompanying capabilities. This moves us from being not much more than a wet noisy pet in infancy to the functional autonomy that's characteristic of adults. A variety of cultural systems that range from the informality of parenting to the formality of classroom instruction nurture this extended development.

We've long been curious about the nature and proper maintenance of life and about the relative roles that our genetic heritage and early experiences play in determining what we become. The commonly used terms for these factors are *nature* and *nurture*. Nature tells us how to *become* a human being. Nurture shapes our environment and development—and so tells us how to *behave* like a human being. The two concepts thus combine species membership with cultural and individual identity.

As these related issues are central to understanding childhood, and are the subject of considerable scientific research, let's begin our exploration of childhood with them.

THE NATURE OF LIFE

Life is an elusive concept—except that it exists in space and time and requires energy to maintain it. Although space, time, and energy seem like simple, straightforward concepts deeply embedded within human language, all three create contentious cultural controversies related to our understanding of the nature and maintenance of life.

Space in human life is basically about objects and locations. We mentally represent these as nouns, qualify them with adjectives, and locate them with spatial prepositions (such as *under, over,* and *within*). A key current spatial issue in biology focuses on where life exists. Is it a property of the entire organism, or does it reside within organs, tissues, cells, or complex molecules such as **DNA**?

Time in human life is basically about events. We mentally represent these as verbs, qualify them with adverbs, and locate them with temporal prepositions (such as *before, during,* and *after*). Key current temporal issues in biology focus on the beginning and ending of life. Are embryonic stem cell research and cloning appropriate? Are capital punishment and assisted suicide appropriate?

Energy in human life is basically about nutrient intake and cognitive arousal and focus beyond basal levels. Our **emotion** and attention systems process arousal and focus. A key current issue focuses on the source of life's energy. Is it centered within self-organizing biological systems that seek and process nutrients, or does it involve such disembodied concepts as mind, spirit, soul, and/or god? Further, is life a discrete variable—something that either exists or doesn't—or is it a continuous spectrum defined by some properties, such as circulation and respiration, that are functional at birth, and others, such as walking and talking, that emerge later?

The Cell

We can think of the cell as the basic structural and functional unit of an organism. The cell provides a space-time-energy identity to a discrete packet of biological information that would otherwise float around aimlessly. The functional concept of *cell* also provides us with an intriguing metaphor for understanding life at several levels, including childhood.

A cell is functionally composed of (1) a protective semipermeable membrane that envelops internal cellular materials but that also contains channels that allow for the selective in-out movement of nutrients and cell products, (2) the cell's nutrient material (cytoplasm), and (3) various processing and regulatory structures—principally a nucleus that contains the cell's long, coiled DNA molecule that provides the genetic directions for **protein** synthesis. The human body has an estimated 100 trillion cells.

Various cellular processes regulate an organism's metabolism. They break down food into useful nutrients that they then use to construct body parts and provide our brain with the chemicals it needs. Cells that are functionally related to each other combine to form tissues and organs. Some of these multicellular systems serve structural or protective roles (e.g., bones, skin, fingernails, kidneys), some process nutrients (e.g., lungs, intestines, liver), and some move nutrients and information (e.g., blood vessels, **neurons**).

From Cell to Body. An entire body has functional parallels to a cell. Our body's version of a cell's semipermeable membrane is our six-pound, 22-square-foot mantle of skin that keeps our insides in place, heat in, and infection out. A cell's membrane has channels that regulate the input and output of materials—and our body has selective sensory and immune systems that recognize external dangers and opportunities, selective digestive and genital systems that serve as in-out conduits for nutrient and reproductive materials, and a language system that receives and sends psychological information.

The constant need for nutrients is a problem for both a cell and an organism, so both tend to take in more than they currently need. The excess is stored for later use—within cellular cytoplasm, for a cell, and within our body as fat and as nutrients that circulate within our bloodstream. Our brain similarly stores experience as retrievable memories and potential problem-solving strategies.

Genetic processes (such as DNA and **RNA**) regulate cellular activity. Their principal tasks are to maintain the cell and build proteins out of the nutrient materials that enter the cell, and then to distribute cellular products for appropriate body use. Our brain is our body's equivalent of these cellular regulatory processes. It receives initially meaningless sensory information, organizes it into an integrated, coherent model of what's occurring inside and outside our body, and then determines an appropriate response.

From Cell to Classroom. A classroom similarly parallels this simple biological model. For example, a classroom's version of a cell's semipermeable membrane includes the walls, windows, doors, faucets, outlets, and so on that surround the inhabitants and regulate the in-/outflow of students and information. Its cache of *nutrients* includes currently used and unused equipment and materials—and hopefully eager-to-learn students (think analogously of **amino acids** in a cell waiting to be organized into proteins so that they can leave the cell and do something useful). The metaphoric equivalent of the cellular nucleus is the teacher and curriculum that combine to organize the school lives of students so that they will personally and intellectually move well beyond their current developmental level.

Childhood as a concept similarly has protective parental and cultural shields around it that help determine what can and should enter into the lives of children. What enters are various controlled forms of nutrient and sensory information that the child's body and brain must organize for immediate or long-term use. Parenting and various forms of teaching help children understand the otherwise confusing positive and negative inputs they receive. What goes out of a child is behavior that is hopefully appropriate and has at least some adult oversight and direction.

What we thus have is a simple but excellent universal model for biological systems. It functions from the level of individual cells to the level of social groups, and it incorporates antecedents (nature) and immediacy (nurture): a protective semipermeable membrane, an extensive collection of potentially useful but currently unorganized and unused materials, and an efficient organizing agent. Life itself!

BIOLOGICAL RANGE

Life exists within ranges, which makes it much more interesting than if everything was identical and unchanging. For example, the hundreds of leaves on a maple tree are easily identified as maple leaves, but no two of them are identical in size, shape, or color. Nor are the arrangements of branches and roots of several nearby maple trees identical. Similarly, all dogs are biologically related, but breeds and individual dogs vary considerably.

Humans function within biologically possible and culturally appropriate ranges. For example, Olympic track records identify the current upper end of the human running range, and posted traffic speeds identify the upper end of the appropriate automobile speed range.

One advantage of having an extended childhood and adolescence is that it allows young people to develop their various capabilities at an individual rate within broadly acceptable ranges. Schools typically work with groups of students, so it's simpler for educators to organize students into developmentally similar groups. Schools use age as the principal grouping criterion during childhood, and interest and capability as the principal criteria during adolescence—but the assumption is that variation within a range will exist and is developmentally appropriate. Grades assess and report how students perform within such assumed ranges.

Conversely, parents focus principally on their own child's development, providing both the **genes** and jeans, as it were. They informally assess such development through observations of their child's peers and through the lens of conventional wisdom about the capabilities of children at various levels of development. I suspect that many also compare their child to their own adult capabilities and to recollections of their own childhood capabilities.

What emerges therefore are two legitimate perspectives: (1) the school's view of the students as members of a peer group and (2) the parents' view of their child as an individual student within a group. Nature provides us with the basic similarities that define a group, and nurture provides us with the striving that characterizes individuals.

NATURE AND NURTURE

Our parents' initial gift to us at conception is the set of about 30,000 **genes** that assemble and regulate our body. Parental egg and sperm combine at conception to produce a long, convoluted, periodically split, ladder-shaped molecule within the initial cell's nucleus—a molecule that is then replicated in all subsequent body cells (except egg, sperm, and red blood cells). It's called deoxyribonucleic acid, DNA for short. DNA is divided into discrete segments called genes, and each functional gene prescribes the length and sequence of the chain of amino acids that make up a specific protein. Proteins provide the scaffolding and machinery of our body's cells, and so they define much of our physical self.

Twenty different kinds of amino acids are all that's needed to make an infinite variety of proteins, just as only 26 letters can construct the 500,000 (and counting) words in the English language. The sequence of amino acids or letters and the length of the chain determine the information, and not the limited numbers of amino acids or letters themselves. The completely different words *do, dog, god, good,* and *goods* demonstrate how this marvelously adaptable coding system creates complex information out of a few simple elements.

This sequential coding system is also used in the small number of tones in musical scales that can create an infinite number of melodies, in the 10 digits of our numeration system that can represent limitless quantities, and in the relatively small number of basic movements that can create many complex actions (such as in the sequence: reach, grasp, elevate, retract, tip, drink).

Just as sequences of words make sentences, stories, and songs, so various genetic combinations result in such basic but complex human properties as gender; body shape; skin, hair, and eye color; and temperament. About nine months after conception, parents discover how their combined genetic directions turned out, and they're usually pleased. We love our babies, who tend to resemble us, but who definitely depend on us to take care of them.

Thirty thousand genes are enough to direct the development and initial operation of a basic birth body, but they're not enough to provide specific directions for living out our complex extended life. Parents must thus provide their child with a second set of instructions—how to transform genetic beginnings into a qualitative cultural life. Their child's extended family, peers, schools, and mass media assist in this nurturing task, and language (with its functional similarities to the genetic code) plays a central role in this process.

As indicated above, the nature/nurture issue revolves around the relative levels of influence that genetic inheritance (nature) and our life experiences (nurture) play in determining our traits and capabilities—in effect, the person we become.

Genetics (nature) activates such conditions as Down syndrome, and it influences such body properties as height and shape; however, the mother's dietary behavior during pregnancy (nurture) and a person's diet and exercise throughout life can alter such basic genetic plans. Genes similarly regulate the development of brain structures, so such cognitive functions as movement, language, and memory also have a genetic base, but experience constantly alters the current organization of a brain's networks and its synaptic connections.

Further, the nature/nurture issue has political overtones. Those who believe that nature is the primary influence in who we become are typically less inclined to support massive programs that hope to improve human conditions they feel can't really be changed. They say, in effect, "Accept your abilities and limitations, and we'll do our best to create a broad accepting society that can accommodate a wide range of capabilities and personalities."

Those who believe that nurture is the primary influence in a person's maturation and lifestyle typically support social service and education programs, especially those that help folks at the lower ends of various human attainment scales. They say, in effect, "Imagine a goal, strive toward it, and our society will help you to achieve it."

What scientists now understand is that neither extreme position is correct. Some human properties, such as height and skin color, are genetically determined and almost impossible to change, but other properties, such as the language we speak and the cultural rituals we follow, are almost entirely based on experience.

One could generalize that genetics is probably more important early in life and environment in later life. However, as suggested above, a woman's use of alcohol and other drugs during pregnancy can affect the development of the fetus (as in fetal alcohol syndrome), and a genetic predisposition to an illness (such as Huntington's disease) could activate later in life regardless of how the person has lived.

Gender orientation has become politically and culturally contentious in recent years, and it's also typically a concern of parents as they observe their children mature. Five to ten percent of the population identify themselves as homosexual. The major current issue is whether the rights and benefits that automatically accrue to married heterosexual couples should also be extended to bonded homosexual couples who wish to marry. Implicit in this is whether our gender orientation is genetically determined or freely chosen.

The scientific evidence currently suggests that, like many other complex human behaviors, some portion of our gender identity is biologically determined, but it's not yet certain what the division is—and how much of it is genetic and epigenetic (affected by hormonal action during pregnancy).

It's also not certain what difference such a determination would currently make, as cultural acceptance occurs much more slowly than the related developments in science and technology. For example, during my elementary school years, teachers vigorously (but ineffectively) urged my left-handed classmates to become right-handed, because a strong cultural bias toward right-handedness existed. Educators no longer do this.

HERITABILITY

Scientists use a measure called heritability that statistically estimates how much nature and nurture contribute to the individual variation observable in a trait. For example, are differences in susceptibility to an illness more related to family lineage or to environmental factors (such as diet or environmental pollutants)? Scientists compare the total amount of variation in susceptibility within a population with the level of susceptibility within specific families. If relatively few people in the general population are susceptible to the illness, but those within certain family groups are much more susceptible, the vulnerability to the illness would be considered heritable.

On the other hand, if you are a member of a family of loggers, your chances of being injured in a logging accident are higher than in the general population, but that type of susceptibility wouldn't be considered heritable. Fingerprint patterns are thus considered heritable, but calluses are occupational (or environmental).

If a trait is said to be 70% heritable, it means that 70% of the observed variation in that trait within a specific sample of people can be attributed to genetic variations among individuals.

It's probably best to think of genes as phenomena that enable rather than constrain behavior. Genes provide the mechanisms for biological *possibility*, but the challenges we confront and the decisions we make determine which genes are expressed to facilitate our responses—and so to affect such human properties as character and intelligence. Ridley (2000) suggests that we thus might better replace the conventional nature *versus* nurture perspective with a more collaborative nature *via* nurture perspective.

Parents and educators can't change the genetic history of a child, but they can do the kind of nurturing that will provide the child with the best possible adaptations of whatever nature provided.

They can also become part of the extended *nurturing* process that needs to occur at the societal level. Most people don't understand the subtle complexities of genetics, but we're all increasingly drawn into moral and political controversies over genetics-related issues. Indeed, recent developments in such areas as **stem cells** and cloning will certainly exacerbate an already contentious discussion of the cultural appropriateness of such research. The resolution of such nature/nurture issues in our democratic society will involve many voters and politicians who unfortunately don't really understand the underlying science implicit in the decisions they'll have to make. Developing a biologically literate society won't occur immediately, but if we delay the beginning, we'll also delay the completion of this important task.

Begin with the children you nurture.

Mastering
Movement

From Imitation to Exploration

Childhood development occurs within our entire body, but much of childhood nurturing occurs during conversations between adult and juvenile brains. A mature plant doesn't nurture its germinated seeds, however, and brainless plants are as biologically successful as animals, so what's the point of a brain?

The principal reason that animals have a brain and plants don't is because animals can move of their own volition and plants can't. Rooted plants aren't going anywhere, so they don't even need to know where they are. What's the point of knowing that other plants have better access to sunlight and water, or that a logger is approaching, if you can't do anything about it?

However, if an organism has legs, wings, or fins, it needs a sensory system to provide information about here and there, a decision-making system to determine if here is better than there or there is better than here, a motor system to get it to there if that's the better option, and a memory system to get back to here after its trip.

Here and there are about space, but our brain also needs to integrate space with time. Movement not only requires the expenditure of energy across space but also over the time it takes to plan and execute movements. Objects and events move slowly or quickly, continuously or intermittently. A brain is thus a system that uses energy to integrate space and time in the regulation of movement—and of life, for all that.

It all begins with a typically pleasant trip of a sperm in search of an egg. Nine months later, our exit trip through our mother's birth canal and the severing of our umbilical cord signal the beginning of an increasingly independent life of movement in all its glorious complexities. Our basic equipment for this journey through life is a three-part motor system—a leg/foot/toe system at the bottom that's about half our body's length and allows us to physically move from here to there and to kick things; an arm/hand/finger system in the middle that extends our reach about two feet and allows us to grasp, carry, throw, and write; and a neck/face/tongue system at the top that initiates digestion and activates a rhythmic flow of air molecules that move linguistic and musical information between and among brains.

These motor systems are excellent but finite. Humans have thus added technological extensions—such as shoes, ladders, wheels, boats, and airplanes—to increase the range and speed of our leg/foot/toe system; hammers, pliers, screwdrivers, gloves, grocery carts, guns, and pencils to increase the capabilities of our arm/hand/finger system; and knives, blenders, cooking, binoculars, microphones, and language to increase the capabilities of our neck/face/tongue system.

Much of our childhood is spent in the development and mastery of personal and technological motor skills. Children seem to intuitively know that if they hope to drive a car at 16, they better get on a tricycle at three. They have to master the integration of perception, arms, and legs in the control of wheels before their parents will give them the keys to the family car. They thus happily spend many hundreds of practice hours on bicycles and skateboards to master wheeled movement in natural space and time.

Similarly, 21st-century children seem to intuitively know that they also have to master movement in cyber space and time. Video game controls are the electronic equivalent of tricycles, and children typically begin to play with the controls of simple games at about three. They seem to realize that they have to master the finite world of game controls and children's video games before they can explore the more complex adult video games and the infinity of the Internet.

But how do children begin the process of learning the myriad of such intentional movements that they must master? For example, if a mother sticks out her tongue at her observant infant a few hours after birth, the infant will intuitively reciprocate without any conscious knowledge of what a tongue is or prior experience with the complex act of projecting a tongue.

The same is true of other early imitative behaviors, such as smiling and clapping hands. Further, many motor skills must begin to develop almost immediately, and most complex motor skills (such as tying a pair of shoes) can't be learned solely through verbal directions.

So although effective movement is our brain's defining property, much of the underlying neurobiology of its activation and mastery was an enigma until recently, when **mirror neurons** were discovered.

MIRROR NEURONS

Most human movement is made up of a relatively few basic motor sequences that can be differentially combined and repeated into many actions. For example, our arm reaches out as our fist opens and closes to grasp a glass of water that we then retract to our mouth and tip. As indicated in Chapter 1, language involves saying or writing specific verbal sequences, such as the letters in *dog* and *god* or the words in the sentences *Bill hit Mary,* as opposed to *Mary hit Bill.* The five-element *reach, grasp, elevate, retract, tip* motor sequence can be represented with a five-element letter sequence—*d-r-i-n-k.* The sequence of elements is central in both cases, and each basic movement or letter may be used as an element of many other actions or words.

Our brain contains myriads of **neural networks** that store and retrieve memories of general and specific facts, personal experiences, and motor sequences. We automatically execute frequently used motor sequences, such as grasping a glass, even though glass sizes differ, but we shift from such automatic behaviors to consciously executed variations if the immediate task is sufficiently different from the mastered skill.

Think of an airplane pilot, who consciously takes off and lands the plane and simply monitors flight events when the computerized automatic pilot is guiding the plane. If a weather front or some other problem arises, the pilot resumes conscious control until the problem is resolved. We often experience an analogous situation when our car is on cruise control and we're carrying on a conversation with a passenger. The conversation briefly stops when something in the road ahead suggests that we should shift from cruise to conscious control of the car and focus our attention completely on driving.

Suffice it to say at this point that several brain systems collaborate in learning, planning, and executing conscious and automatic movements. Two systems important to understanding mirror neurons and intentional movement are the **motor cortex,** which activates the specific muscles involved in a motor sequence, and the **premotor area** of the **frontal lobes,** which remembers and primes the motor sequence.

Giacomo Rizzolatti (Rizzolatti & Sinigaglia, 2007) and his team of Italian neuroscientists discovered mirror neurons in the early 1990s. They were studying the brain systems that regulate intentional hand movements in monkeys. They discovered that neurons in the premotor areas of the **cortex** that remember and prime motor sequences (such as how to grasp an object or to break open a peanut) activate milliseconds before the motor cortex neurons fire and the action occurs. The relevant premotor system thus forms an action sequence that activates the relevant motor cortex system that activates the relevant muscles.

What amazed the scientists was the discovery one day that this premotor system also activates when their monkey simply observed someone else making that same intentional movement.

These premotor neurons don't activate at the mere observation of a hand or mouth—only when it is carrying out a goal-directed action. Further, they respond to a hand but not to a tool that is grasping or moving an object because a brain's motor areas regulate body parts and not tools. When the target of an action is an object (such as picking up a peanut) certain **parietal lobe** neurons are also activated. Scientists called this system the mirror neuron system.

This discovery was very significant because it identified the brain systems that create a mental template of an observed intentional movement of someone else, and then prime the responsive imitative behavior. They don't in themselves generate the response, but rather they enhance its probability. In effect, mirror neurons connect the subjective worlds of the actor and observer.

A cognitive system that allows a brain to automatically simulate and then to imitate the observed goal-directed movements of others would thus be an ideal learning system for complex movements, and that's the critically important role that mirror neurons play in the maturation of a brain's movement capabilities.

After the initial monkey research, neuroscientists used **neuroimaging technologies** to study mirror neurons in humans. They discovered that we have an incredibly complex mirror neuron system that encompasses our entire sensory and perceptual systems, allowing us to both simulate and empathize with the emotional lives and intentional states of others, driving our rich communicative and cultural life. Mirror neurons are thus central to our very existence as a social species, because our immature birth brain must master many motor skills during childhood.

When we observe someone yawn, it activates our brain's yawning program. Adults typically override the tendency and stifle the yawn; however, as indicated above, if we stick out our tongue at an infant who is only a few hours old, it's probable that she will immediately reciprocate even though she had never before stuck out her tongue or even has any conscious awareness of it. The chances are good, however, that it's the fetal muscle she exercised the most by sucking her thumb.

Her observation of our behavior will automatically activate the mirror neurons that prime the motor neurons that activate her tongue projection movements. She has a zillion movements to learn and therefore no reason to stifle the action. Similarly, smile, and she'll smile. Clap your hands, and she'll clap her hands. The statement *monkey see, monkey do* also relates nicely to human infants.

Life would be chaotic, however, if the extended human mirror neuron system was simply a subconscious automatic system that imitated every observed intentional action. Our brain must thus rapidly determine if it's simply enough to know the state of another person (and so to stifle a yawn) or to reciprocate a movement sequence (such as when someone initiates a handshake or a hug). A common communicated understanding about what's important and appropriate must therefore exist in both the actor and the observer.

Communication. As indicated above, language is a key form of human movement. It's probable that mirror neurons helped to expand human communication from gestural to vocal sequences. We can use our legs to approach a friend and extend our hand for a handshake greeting, but we can also stay where we are and project rhythmic air patterns via mouth and tongue movements. These sequential sound patterns activate ear and brain activity that our friend interprets as a verbal greeting. Written language and music are thus also forms of communicative movement.

We can observe the friendly movements of a handshake, but we cannot see what's occurring inside a speaker's mouth, where speech sounds are regulated. The mirror neuron system helps to explain how a child learns to speak.

Our sensorimotor system is highly interconnected, so we can visualize a named but nonvisible object, such as when someone says *banana*. Similarly, hearing articulate speech activates the same speech-production processes in the child's brain that the speaker used to sequence the sounds and words. This process is enhanced through *Motherese*, a universal behavior in which an adult holds an infant in a close face-on-face position; and then speaks in a slowed-down, high-pitched, exaggerated, repetitive, melodic format that engages the infant's attention and easily activates her mirror neuron system. Speech is a complex motor activity, so the infant initially *babbles* in incoherent imitation; but, over time, in a verbal environment, the child begins to correctly utter simple phonemic combinations . . . and eventually, smooth articulate speech emerges.

We often use gestures to accompany conversational and presentational speech. The gestures supplement and enhance the meaning, rhythmic pattern, and emotional overtones of what we say. Mirror neuron involvement in the process is evident when observers overtly or covertly imitate the speaker's gestures. Mimicked gestures are also integral to many children's songs and games.

When we observe someone in the initial stages of a movement sequence, such as when a diner picks up a knife and fork, we infer the subsequent actions because our brain is *mirroring* the entire common movement sequence and so *knows* what will occur next. When a speaker stops midsentence, we can often complete the sentence.

Think of how your computer will complete a frequently used e-mail or website address after you type the first few letters. Our brain similarly remembers entire movement sequences.

This probably also explains why most people consider it more difficult to give a formal speech than to engage in a conversation. Two brains work together easily when exploring an idea conversationally. They infer, build on, and complete each other's thoughts in an informal manner that allows the conversation to meander as it will.

This ability to infer the direction of an observed behavior is also important for adults who are supervising children. When we observe a child in the initial stages of inappropriate or risky behavior, we can anticipate the probable result and intervene before it's too late.

Athletes *fake out* an opponent's mirror neuron system by beginning an action, and then quickly and unexpectedly switching to a different action. Magicians use the same switching technique to fool their audience. A continued untrue explanation may similarly place hearers into a mirrored mental state in which the deception eventually seems reasonable.

Ballroom dancing, musical duets, and tennis matches are a few of the many examples of social interaction in which partners enjoy the mirrored activity of unspoken communication.

Empathy and Compassion. Because our brain's hundreds of processing systems are highly interconnected, mirror neurons not only simulate the actions of others but also their related properties, such as the pain or pleasure that can result from an observed action. The anterior **cingulate** and **insula** are frontal lobe systems that process pain, and mirror neurons in these systems respond to the observed pain that others are experiencing (typically communicated through facial expressions and body language). This leads to empathy and compassion, essential components for successful human interaction. The term *empathy* describes our ability to internalize and so understand the emotional state of another person, and *compassion* describes the feelings we have for the plight of that person.

Empathy and compassion can further emerge through third-party reports, such as news reports of the victims of natural disasters or accidents. We will almost always instantly recall and relive any similar experience we had.

Virtuoso Performance. Mirror neurons may also help to explain why so many of us enjoy observing and predicting the movements of virtuoso athletes, dancers, and musicians. Virtuoso performances allow our mirror neuron system to mentally model (and thus enjoy) actions that we can't physically mimic at that level of performance. Mirror neurons become more active as we gradually master a skill by observing those who are better at it than we are.

Children spend a lot of time observing and imitating the actions of older children who have mastered the movements they seek to master. We often see them standing off from the action but totally engrossed in it.

Note the body language of former athletes who are observing a game—how they actively imitate the movements of the athletes playing the game, and how they can see individual movements within the complexity of the action that the rest of us don't see. Further, athletes frequently use mental imagery to enhance their performance of specific practiced movement sequences.

Metaphor. Metaphoric thought allows us to recognize common properties in seemingly dissimilar entities, such as in a brain and a computer. Because metaphor allows us to connect novel, complex, and abstract phenomena to something we already understand, it's central to such cultural elements as the arts, humanities, and religion.

Movement can also be metaphorical. No two movements are absolutely identical, but they're often sufficiently similar that we recognize classes of movements, such as shooting free throws in basketball. A fouled player can use various techniques to shoot the ball, but it's not considered a free throw if the player doesn't stand at the free throw line or shoots the ball from the free throw line during regular play. It's thus important that our brain understands the requisite properties in comparisons.

The motor skills needed to play a guitar and violin are sufficiently similar so that a person who can play one instrument has an advantage in learning the other instrument over someone who hasn't played either. It's not surprising then that mirror neurons are an element of our metaphoric capabilities.

Several brain systems are probably involved in processing metaphors, and the **angular gyrus** is a likely principal candidate. It's located at the juncture of our sight, sound, and touch processing centers, and it contains mirror neurons.

Children typically begin to explore metaphor within the context of the stories we tell them and the books that they read. For example, many fairy tales and parables contain animals and machines that exhibit human qualities, and such stories typically seek to connect imaginary events with the life of a child.

Electronic Media. The mirror neuron system evidently works best when it directly observes human behavior, but it apparently can also respond to televised and filmed human movements. This poses intriguing currently unresolved issues about the effect of the electronic depiction of violent and sexual behavior on the subsequent real-life behavior of immature observers.

Autism. It now appears that at least some people who suffer from the autism spectrum have a deficient mirror neuron system, and this would explain their inability to infer and empathize with the thoughts and behaviors of others, to comprehend metaphor and proverbs, and to easily master articulate speech. The presumed connection between the malady and mirror neurons opens up promising research possibilities into the diagnosis and eventual treatment of autism. It's also probable that other learning disabilities will also be traced to deficiencies in our mirror neuron system.

An old adage suggests that children attend more to what we do than to what we say. If so, our mirror neuron system may eventually explain the effectiveness of many traditional teaching and parenting techniques in which explicit modeling provides children with an effective behavioral pattern to follow. For example, working with children on a task such as mixing and baking a cake at home or mixing papier-mâché paste at school encourages the imitative behaviors that mirror neurons mediate.

At another level, classroom chalkboards are increasingly being replaced by newer technologies such as PowerPoint presentations. It's perhaps an inevitable change, but PowerPoint information tends to appear full blown on the screen, as opposed to the students' observation of the teacher's arm movements and body language as a diagram, algorithm, or text gradually emerges on a chalkboard or overhead screen. Some technological developments in teaching might thus diminish traditional teacher behaviors that are developmentally significant in ways that we didn't formerly realize.

Mirror neurons may thus provide us with key elements of the neurobiological base of 21st-century theories of teaching and parenting. The renowned neuroscientist V. S. Ramachandran (2006) suggested that the discovery of mirror neurons might provide the same powerful unifying framework for our understanding of teaching and learning that the 1953 discovery of DNA did for our understanding of genetics.

MASTERING MOVEMENT

An extended sheltered human maturation permits children and adolescents to gradually and informally develop competence in basic motor skills and to explore the wide variety of challenges and solutions that independent life will later present. Such learning generally emerges through various forms of *play* and *games* that continue the developmental process begun with mirror neurons. The mastery of most motor skills requires considerable practice, which must be in the form of sufficiently pleasant experiences for the child to continue doing them.

Play involves informal individual or small-group explorations of motor skills with a minimal focus on a clearly defined goal. Play has a joy about it that communicates the pure exuberance of movement for its own sake. At some developmental point, however, young people want to compare their motor and decision-making abilities with that of others, and games do that.

Games are the more-organized and typically scored comparisons of specific skills exhibited by competing individuals or teams who have the same clearly defined goal. Skilled movement involves the ability to plan actions, to regulate movements during the action, and to predict the movements of others and objects. Games typically require success in all three tasks, and these reach their peak in such events as the Olympic Games, which seek to identify the best athletes in the world in selected motor skills. It's important to note, however, that games don't necessarily involve intense physical movement. Chess is an example of a game that is more cerebral than physical in the planning, regulation, and prediction of its movements.

Children will joyfully spend much personal time and energy on play and games that challenge them to master developmentally important knowledge and skills that relate to problems that intrigue them. In this, they frequently have no conscious awareness of the developmental needs implicit in the activity. For example, the universal childhood fascination for scary stories and games is probably related to the innate need to develop and maintain the systems that process the important **emotion** of fear and its consequent behavioral response, and to develop such systems in nonthreatening settings.

Our primary emotions are fear, anger, disgust, surprise, sadness, and joy, and we can add many secondary and blended emotions to that list (such as anticipation, tension, and pride). All involve the emotionally important cognitive arousal systems that must be developed and maintained for a brain to recognize and subsequently move away from dangers and to move toward opportunities. It's a use-it-or-lose-it proposition.

Some of these emotions may not be sufficiently activated in normal life to help maintain an important but rarely used survival skill. Play and games frequently and artificially activate temporary fear (and its handmaiden, attention), however, and this may partly explain our culture's strong and enduring interest in play and games. Note how all the other emotions (and attention) play similarly key roles in play and games.

The Arts. The arts also play an important role in the development and maintenance of motor skills. We not only want to playfully explore movement, we want to move with style and grace. For example, children seek first to simply master balance and basic movements on a skateboard, but as soon as they feel confident, their interests begin to shift from using the skateboard as merely a means of transportation to the aesthetics of skateboard movement. For all practical purposes, skateboarding becomes a form of dance.

All forms of the arts involve movement, whether it's a painter moving paint to a canvas or the rhythmic beats of a drummer or the raised eyebrow of an actor. We don't merely move to move but also to add aesthetic elements to human life.

Arts experiences that interest us tend to relate to important personal concerns. They thus allow us to explore the topics in a nonthreatening play-like manner during periods when we're not actually confronted by the problem in its real form, and so they help us to develop and maintain the emotion, attention, and problem-solving systems that normally process the challenge.

Physical Education. The recent reductions in school arts and physical education programs and the resulting loss of an atmosphere of play in school are thus a biological tragedy that we'll come to regret when our society matures in its understanding of the central role that physical movement in all of its manifestations plays in the development and maintenance of a child's brain.

Indeed, Ratey (2008) reports credible research studies that indicate how an active physical exercise program can actually improve the curricular attainment and physical well-being of students. For example, the nationally recognized Naperville, Illinois, secondary school exercise program is credited with materially increasing test scores and improving the behavior of students and the culture of the school. Further, only 3% of the 19,000 students are overweight (by body mass indicator standards), as compared to 30% nationwide.

Psychological Movement

We can also think of movement within the context of psychological states, such as moving from infancy to childhood to adolescence to young adulthood to being middle aged to elderly. We move from being unemployed to employed, from unmarried to married. We shift our allegiance from one political or religious belief to another.

We tend to be fascinated by great historical movements. Immigration in its various manifestations has been a long and continuing cultural and political issue in the United States, and the Lewis and Clark Expedition sparked increased internal movement within the country. Most religions commemorate some central movement event—the departure of Adam and Eve from the Garden of Eden, the Jewish Exodus from Egypt, Mohammed's journey from Medina to Mecca, and the Mormon trek to Utah are notable examples.

Literature abounds with the stories of people moving through time and space, from the *Odyssey* to *Moby Dick* to *Harry Potter*. The broad appeal of the Harry Potter series among young people is reflective of the variety of imaginative physical and psychological movements the young characters experience.

Movement is thus a manifestation of life itself. Our bodies teem with movement, even when we think we're immobile. Our hearts are beating and blood is flowing. Our lungs are expanding and contracting. Nutrients are moving through the digestive system. Neural impulses are coursing through our brains. Viral and bacterial invaders are moving about, warily observed by our immune systems. To be perfectly still is to be completely dead.

Teachers who prefer that their students sit still and be quiet are perhaps more interested in teaching a grove of trees than a classroom of students.

Brain Organization

From Input to Output

Our brain has over a trillion highly interconnected **neurons** and **glial support cells.** They're organized into many hundreds of systems and subsystems that collaboratively process various specific elements of our brain's definitive task—to plan, regulate, and predict the responsive movements that are appropriate to the challenges we confront.

Our brain's neurons are specialized cells that move molecular information within and among the neuronal networks that collaborate on cognitive tasks and between our brain and sensorimotor system. This molecular movement creates perception, thought, decision, and behavior.

Several types of glial cells, which make up half the mass of our brain, provide a variety of important neuronal support services.

Although various types of neurons differ somewhat in shape, Figure 3.1 suggests that they basically resemble our finger/hand/arm system. The palm represents the cell body

Figure 3.1   Finger/Hand/Arm—Dendrite/Cell Body/Axon

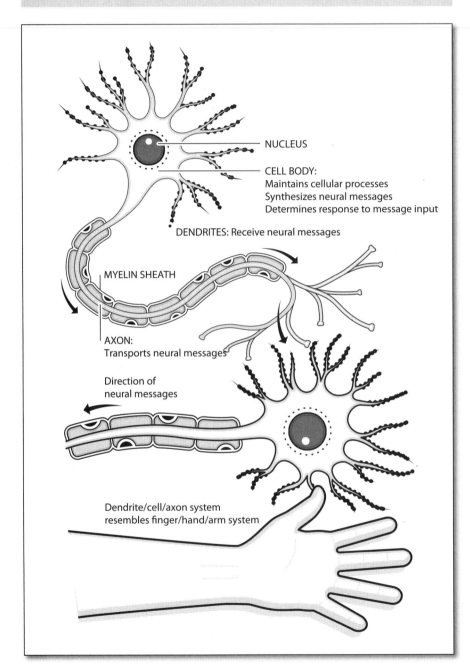

NUCLEUS

CELL BODY:
Maintains cellular processes
Synthesizes neural messages
Determines response to message input

DENDRITES: Receive neural messages

MYELIN SHEATH

AXON:
Transports neural messages

Direction of
neural messages

Dendrite/cell/axon system
resembles finger/hand/arm system

that contains the genetic and nutrient-processing material of a typical body cell. Fingers represent the multiple **dendrite** extensions on a neuron that bring in molecular information from other neurons. The arm represents a neuron's (typically single) **axon** that sends messages from the neural cell body to other neurons within and beyond a neuron's network. A neuron may connect to thousands of nearby and distant neurons. (Appendix A provides additional background information on neurons and glial cells.)

Three major systems predominate in our brain—the sub cortex, the cerebrum, and the cerebellum. The cerebrum is divided into four subsystems that are central to brain maturation—the right and left hemispheres and the paired sensory and frontal lobes.

Our Brain's Functional Organization

Sub Cortex

The **sub cortical area** in and around the finger-size **brainstem** at the base of our brain focuses principally on nutrient movements that occur within our body. It regulates such functions as circulation, respiration, and digestion, and it synthesizes and distributes many of the **neurotransmitters** that move chemical information within and among neural networks.

The sub cortical systems keep us alive by subconsciously maintaining a constant flow of fluids and gases throughout our body. It makes sense because it's obviously impossible to consciously regulate such systems as respiration when we're asleep or are focused on another task. This system's innate automatic nature also eliminates the need for adults to teach a newly born infant how to breathe or how to regulate circulation and digestion. We can, however, consciously override the automatic regulation of these systems when conditions require us to temporarily increase or decrease activity, and that also makes sense.

Figure 3.2   Cortex/Sub Cortex/Cerebellum

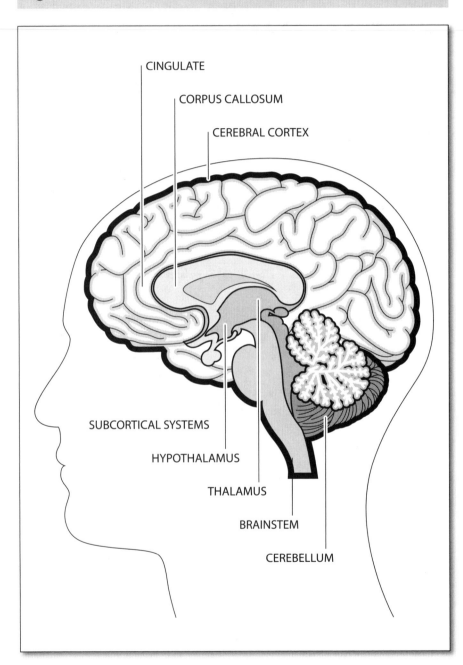

The guiding regulatory principal is that key survival functions must either be innate and automatic (such as circulation), or else they must be easily mastered with limited explicit instruction (such as our ability to walk and talk).

Cerebrum

The **cerebrum** encompasses about 80% of the mass of our brain. It includes the large six-layer-thick cellular sheet of **cortex (gray matter)** and its dense underlying connections (**white matter**) that fold over and around the sub cortical area. The cerebrum's principal task is to process our interactions with the external environment—to recognize and respond to the challenges we constantly confront. The sub cortical area is much smaller than the cerebrum because body functions such as respiration and circulation are repetitive rather than complex, and so their regulatory systems are relatively simple. They need only to establish and maintain a consistent rhythmic pattern. Conversely, the processing systems in the cerebrum must recognize and respond to many complex, ambiguous, and irregular external challenges, and this requires much more neuronal-processing capability.

The cerebral systems function mostly through conscious control because of the variety of challenges we confront and the different responses we might make. Our brain must quickly determine the specific nature of a challenge and then decide which of several possible responses is best. Much of our childhood and adolescence is thus devoted to the maturation of the many complex cerebral systems that regulate conscious behavior. We'll return to the organization of the cerebrum and its four major subsystems later in the chapter.

Cerebellum

The sub cortical and cerebral systems collaborate on many functions, and the **cerebellum** (meaning *little brain*) located behind the brainstem plays a central role in this. It efficiently coordinates the planning, timing, and execution of a variety of complex sensorimotor activities.

Most of us could probably eventually resolve minor computer problems with a good manual, but it's so much better to have a readily available friend who truly understands the nuances of computer technology and is willing to quickly and correctly connect the appropriate systems. Our cerebellum provides an analogous efficient coordinating service for a variety of brain systems that would otherwise function at a much lower efficiency. An acquaintance told me that he considers his computer-whiz adolescent son to be the *cerebellum* of his parents' relationship to computers.

Our brain thus functions via a combination of innate/reflexive and learned/reflective processing systems. This combination has advantages and disadvantages. For example, we have two separate systems that analyze the dangers and opportunities we confront and then determine how best to respond.

1. Challenges with a sense of importance and immediacy are rapidly and reflexively processed by our brain's innate stress-driven, conceptual (principally sub cortical) problem-solving system. This system responds quickly on the basis of the small amount of emotionally intense information that's typically available. It's thus quite vulnerable to making impetuous, racist, sexist, and elitist responses that focus on only a few highly visible emotion-charged elements.

2. Challenges without a sense of immediacy are processed more slowly and reflectively by our brain's curiosity-driven, analytical (principally cerebral) problem-solving system.

We thus will respond *reflexively* to a car that's moving swiftly toward us (conceptually concerned only with its looming rapid approach), but we'll generally respond *reflectively* to a car on a dealer's lot if we're considering its purchase (and are thus concerned with its service history, possible malfunctioning systems, cost, etc.).

Our rapid reflexive system is the default system because it responds to dangers and opportunities that require an immediate decisive (fight/flight) response that will enhance our survival. When it isn't immediately obvious whether a reflexive or reflective response is the more appropriate, both systems simultaneously search for a solution, with the reflexive system typically responding first.

Most of us thus ad hoc our way through life with a long string of regrets and apologies because of the late arrival of our brain's (often better) reflective response.

The problem with children is that they of necessity have functional reflexive systems, but their reflective systems are a work in progress, dependent on the nurturing of parents, teachers, and other adults who will help them learn how to rationally respond to the increasingly complex challenges that emerge during childhood and adolescence. The common (and often biologically appropriate) instant gratification tendencies and fearfulness of young children thus leads them to respond immediately and vociferously to many events that older children and adults consider unimportant or at least rationally negotiable.

Many problems that humans now face don't require an impulsively reflexive response, so the educational and parental challenge is to help children develop and practice their emerging reflective capabilities in a low-threat environment that provides intriguing simulations of challenges that they'll confront as adults. For example, genuinely involving children in a discussion of the necessary preparations for a classroom party or a family vacation introduces them to the way that rational thought and planning occurs, and it provides them with strategies they can retrieve and use when they begin to confront similar problems. It further helps them to analyze televised and other marketing campaigns that use such elements as bright colors, rapid movements, and oscillating sounds to artificially enhance a product's importance, which thus seek a reflexive rather than reflective purchasing decision from consumers.

We can see parallels to our brain's modular collaborative organization within many movement-related social systems. This isn't surprising because an individual brain's capabilities and limitations are similar to those of a collaborative group of brains. The policies and practices of a successful organization thus parallel the properties of an individual brain.

Let's use the game of football as an example of something in which the central task parallels that of a brain—to *plan, regulate, and predict movement*. A university football team with 100 or so players fields 11 players when it's on offense and typically a different set of 11 players when it's on defense. Some players (such as kickers and punt receivers) carry out a single specialized function, and several dozen players substitute for the principal players when necessary. The coaching staff makes many of the decisions that the players execute, and the quarterback is the key team player on offense.

Various constraints apply. The game is played with a ball and within space and time boundaries. Activity is limited to movements that are biologically possible and behaviors that are culturally appropriate (the rules).

Some kinds of game situations occur often, some rarely, and the coaches have to plan for both possibilities. If a given challenge is probable, specific players will enter the game to play specialized responsive roles. If the opponents do something unexpected, the players on the field will have to improvise a response. Small combinations of players from a team of 100 players will thus be able to function effectively in hundreds of possible game situations.

Our brain functions similarly within the constraints of what's biologically possible and culturally appropriate. It can sequence selected combinations of the 26 letters in our alphabet into the half-million words in the English language, and it can further sequence words into sentences and stories. Its hundreds of processing systems function at different levels of specialization and activation. When our brain confronts a challenge, it rapidly sizes up the dynamics of the situation, and the appropriate systems activate in response. If something unexpected occurs, our ability to improvise a response is often dependent on the amount of past experience we've had with similar situations.

For comparison, our brain has separate systems to recognize and respond to challenges, just as a football team has separate teams for defense and offense. Our brain has primary and backup systems that process certain functions, and a football team has first team and substitute players and primary and secondary receivers in a passing play. Our brain has some processing systems that are highly specific in what they do, and it has others that are incorporated into many cognitive activities. A football team similarly has players who specialize in one function and others who are used in many game situations. The goal of all this cognitive activity is an effective appropriate behavior, and the goal of all this athletic activity is yards gained or points scored.

Many other useful brain-culture parallels exist, and therefore one could similarly identify analogous parallels in other games and organizations that a child understands. Our brain is awesomely complex in its biology, but it also has an elegant functional simplicity about it that even children can understand. Therefore, teachers and parents can easily find parallels between a child's brain and many phenomena in nature and society (including the management of a classroom and family). As indicated in Chapter 1, it's important for 21st-century children to begin to understand and think about such parallels if they expect to make informed and appropriate adult decisions on cultural issues related to biology and society.

Our brain's current organization is a result of successful genetic adaptations to a wide range of environmental challenges that occurred over evolutionary time. Conversely, *nature* hasn't had enough generations to adapt to recent cultural and technological developments. The automobile goes back only three generations; television, two generations; and computers, a single generation. *Nurture* thus becomes very important as each brain adapts its innate ancient systems to the specific novel challenges it confronts during its lifetime.

For example, our brain is innately more tuned to life in a small simple community than to a complex urban community, so urban children have to be specifically taught how to cross streets and interact with strangers. Similarly, speaking is innately easier to master than reading and writing (which emerged later). But nurturing adults can help children to respond effectively to both urban life and written language, so a child's behavior in complex challenges can become effective and automatic.

LOCATING CHILDHOOD BEHAVIOR WITHIN OUR BRAIN

Most adult nurturing activity seeks to enhance the effectiveness of processing systems that are either located within the cerebrum (or are directly connected to cerebral systems), so it's helpful to understand the cerebrum's functional constituents and connections.

The Cortex

The unfolded six-layer cerebral cortex is about the size and thickness of a stack of six sheets of 12" × 18" construction paper, and so the stack creates a simple readily available model of the cortex to use when explaining our brain's organization. Place your upright index finger in the middle of the bottom of the stack to represent the brainstem, and think of the other folded fingers of your fist as the cerebellum.

The cortex has both a horizontal and vertical organization, as Figure 3.3 illustrates.

The cortex contains six horizontal layers, each with a distinct pattern of connections, organization, and function. Information entering the cortex from elsewhere in our brain typically enters layer four. The top layers (1–3) move information regionally within the upper layers (think of

Figure 3.3   A Slice of the Cortex Showing the Layers and Columns

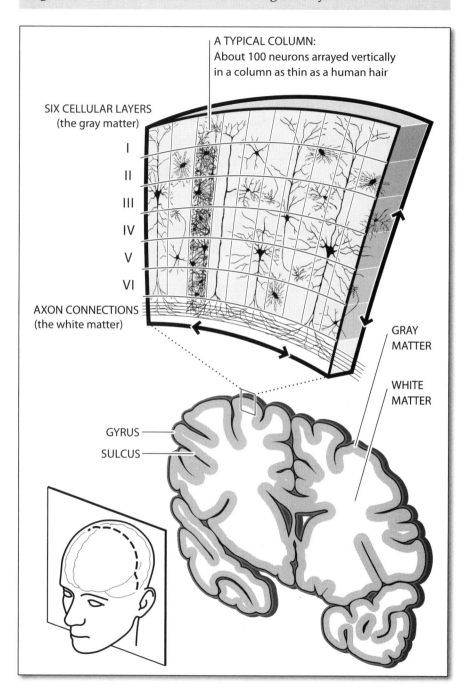

interoffice memos). Communication with more-distant brain and body systems tends to emerge out of the bottom layers (5 and 6).

The vertical organization of the cortex involves hundreds of millions of highly interconnected columns of about 100 neurons that extend vertically through the six cortical layers (the gray matter). Each set of related columns is specialized to process a very specific unit of information (such as to recognize a diagonal line or a specific tone or to move a specific finger joint).

The axons of columnar neurons in the lower layers extend into the white matter, a dense web of axon connections beneath the gray matter. The axons eventually leave the white matter to connect with neuronal dendrites in a related nearby or distant column or to project into noncolumnar brain, sensory, or muscle systems.

Thus, discrete columnar brain areas and systems process basic limited cognitive functions. These are incorporated into larger, specialized, widely distributed but highly interconnected areas and systems that collaborate on complex cognitive tasks. For example, our visual system has about 30 separate columnar subsystems that process such visual properties as shape, depth, color, quantity, and movement. The subsystem that responds to the color red processes it on every red object we see, and the subsystem that responds to circular shapes processes balls, CDs, tires, donuts, and so on. Several of these subsystems will thus combine to process our perception of a single red ball rolling across a table.

The axons that form and connect neural networks (the white matter) were long viewed as mere passive tissue—as roads that merely move information among gray matter areas where *the real cognitive work* supposedly occurs. The cellular decision to send information from one brain system to another does indeed occur within the columnar gray matter, but the white matter coordinates the intricate movement of signals from various distances so that they arrive in the right place at the right time. **Myelin,** a covering over longer axons that enhances transmission, is a central element in this coordination.

Roads are designed and built to reflect the traffic demands of a given area, and the developmental pattern of white matter similarly reflects the challenges and experiences of a brain. Confronting the challenges of instruction in a skill (such as in music and sports) during childhood develops a more robust connecting system that correlates with how well we can process the related skill as an adult. Similarly, elevated levels of white matter correlate with higher IQ levels in young people.

A simple metaphor will help you and children to understand the division and organization of our brain's hundreds of processing systems, many of which are innately dedicated to a specific important task and most of which aren't active at any given time.

Think of a 100-neuron column (in the gray matter) as containing the information in a 100-page book, and its axonal white matter (that connects with other neurons) as the bibliography that connects the information in that book to other books. Further, think of the entire cerebral cortex as a library, the columns as shelved library books, and the processing systems that encompass the cerebral cortex as the various library areas (that contain books and other information on history, science, etc.).

Library-shelf areas are thus assigned to a given category of books, such as fiction in one library area and science in another. A student would generally gather information from several books in a given area while preparing a report on that topic, and she would ignore library areas and books unrelated to the research topic. Our brain similarly efficiently gathers the information it needs from various brain areas specialized to provide the needed information or function and doesn't activate other unrelated areas.

Important library topics have more shelf space devoted to them than less important topics, but the library's shelf space can be reorganized to accommodate an expanding collection of books in any category. Dedicated neuronal systems can similarly recruit neurons from less dedicated surrounding areas if they need more power to process their task. Scientists can observe this developing spatial inequality in the larger amount of motor cortex space dedicated to coordinating movement in a person's dominant arm/hand as compared to the other, or in the expansion of neuronal space devoted to left-hand digital capabilities when a right-handed person becomes a violin student.

This altering of the connecting patterns of neurons and systems of neurons is called **plasticity**. It's obviously a central element of parenting, teaching, and learning, and it occurs throughout life as we adapt to new challenges. How the biological neuronal realignments actually occur is the focus of much current research. The functionally important thing for those who work with children to realize is that every behavioral change is the result of a biological change.

Another simple metaphor can help to explain the utility of the horizontal and vertical organization of the cortex. Think of the individual people who make up a community as being the vertical columns in the cortex. Each person plays a unique role in community life, just as each cortical column processes a unique element of our body or the environment (flexing an elbow or recognizing the elbow shape of macaroni). Each person is unique, but all people in the community have common properties; for example, they use their legs at the bottom of their bodies to move from here to there; their arms and hands in the middle of their bodies to grasp, carry, throw, and so on; and their heads at the top of their bodies to eat, see, talk, and so forth. So, if we line up a group of people, we can see a horizontal organization (legs/hands/heads) that implies their human similarities, and we see a vertical organization that implies each person's uniqueness in the community. The cortex similarly has a middle layer that takes in information, a top trio of layers that communicates principally with adjacent areas, and a bottom pair of layers that send messages to other brain and body areas.

THE CEREBRAL HEMISPHERES

The right and left hemispheres are the two major divisions of the cerebrum. They are separated by a deep longitudinal cerebral fissure, and they are connected by axons that comprise the underlying **corpus callosum** and **anterior commissure**.

Conscious thought and action are primarily processed in the two cerebral hemispheres. The symmetrically paired systems of many animals, such as eyes, ears, legs, wings, thumbs, kidneys, and cerebral hemispheres, provide decided advantages. Paired muscles and limbs obviously allow animals to move more rapidly and efficiently, and having two systems provides a backup in case one becomes disabled. Further, many tasks require the coordination of two related systems—one leg balances our body while the other kicks a ball; one hand holds a sheet of paper while the other cuts it with scissors.

Our two cerebral hemispheres have different processing assignments and so are organized differently, but they typically function as an efficient integrated unit because they are so highly interconnected. Think of a married couple who have determined the primary responsibility for each of various family and household tasks, but who constantly collaborate in solving family problems. They thus perceive themselves as a *coupled* unit. We can similarly perceive our unified *self* as something that emerges from the collaborative actions of the paired hemispheres.

Hemispheres, Left and Right

Scientists have identified functions that seem to be processed principally in one hemisphere, such as language and numerical computation in the left hemisphere and spatial ability and face recognition in the right hemisphere. This poses the problem of what purpose the left hemisphere serves in nonhuman primates, as they don't process articulate language or master the multiplication tables. Goldberg (2005) suggests an alternative hemispheric organizing principle.

Because responding effectively to looming dangers and opportunities is an important cognitive task, the fundamental organizing principle for the right and left hemispheres emerged out of an important question a brain must answer before deciding how to respond to a challenge: Have I confronted this problem before?

Goldberg argues that the right hemisphere (in most humans) is organized to effectively interpret and creatively respond to novel challenges, and the left hemisphere is organized to identify familiar challenges and then activate effective responses developed during previous, related challenges. The right hemisphere neuronal systems are thus broadly connected to permit the consideration of many alternatives. The left hemisphere systems are connected for rapid efficient processing. Musically naïve people process music principally in their right hemisphere, trained musicians in the left.

The initial solution to a novel challenge doesn't necessarily have to be the best solution—just something that works well enough to keep us alive. We then save that solution as a memory, recall and adapt it for use the next time we confront a similar problem, and then save that solution as a memory. Think of the similar way in which we save the successful drafts of a manuscript (and delete earlier drafts) until it becomes just what we want it to be.

Although both hemispheres are active in processing most cognitive functions, the relative level of involvement thus shifts from the right to the left hemisphere over time as we become increasingly familiar with the challenge, more competent at resolving it, and more secure in our interpretation of related issues. The right hemisphere is thus organized to rapidly and creatively respond to a novel challenge, but the more linear organization of the left hemisphere eventually translates the successful initial responses into an efficient established routine that is quickly activated whenever the challenge reoccurs.

All of this makes sense. Grammatical language is an efficient, sequential, established system for enhancing communication within a socially complex species, so it's not surprising that considerable left hemisphere space is devoted to it. A dependent infant uses whatever nonverbal communication skills it can creatively muster to get the help it needs, but then it spends much of its childhood mastering the much more efficient existing cultural language template that we pass from generation to generation.

It's probably important to add that the left hemisphere processes the primary meaning of a word, while the right hemisphere processes its context and connotations—everything that's typically omitted in a dictionary definition, such as the emotional overtones of a sentence or metaphor. The complexities of language are such that our brain must simultaneously process both the *forest* (right hemisphere) and the individual *trees* (left hemisphere), as it were.

The broader neuronal connectivity in the right hemisphere thus enhances the awareness of the subtler and far-reaching relationships in a challenge, and this can result in such phenomena as insight. This is probably why we often develop a sudden insightful solution to a problem while we're relaxed and not focusing on it. Our right hemisphere systems continue to consider alternatives while our left hemisphere is focused on something else. Our brain's executive systems (in some currently ill-understood manner) will instantly recognize an appropriate insightful resolution to a problem and pop it up into conscious awareness.

The world children confront is predominantly novel, so their dominant right hemisphere is willing to consider all sorts of possibilities. Santa Claus and the Tooth Fairy can seem reasonable to a right hemisphere. The school's focus on left hemisphere analysis, precision, and efficiency might thus reduce a student's interest in and ability to develop insightful solutions to problems that already have a conventional solution.

The Cerebral Lobes

Each hemisphere is divided into four lobes, as shown in Figure 3.4. Each lobe has a principal assignment, but it also carries out other tasks and, as indicated above, a lot of collaboration among lobes occurs on almost every cognitive task.

Figure 3.4   Side View of the Cerebrum Identifying the Lobes

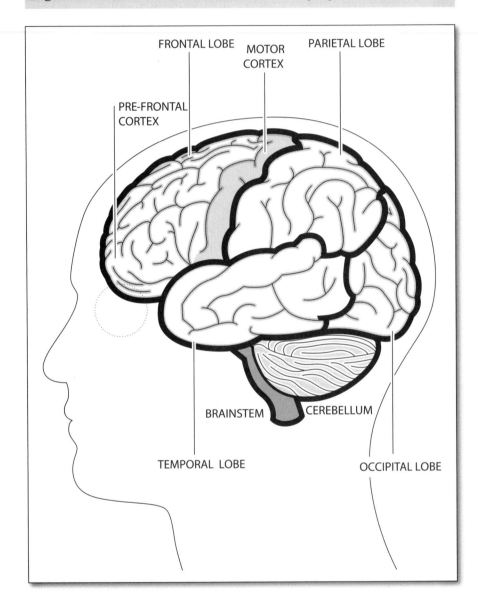

The three lobes in the back half receive and analyze incoming sensory information (**occipital**/sight, **temporal**/hearing, and parietal/touch) and integrate the various forms of information into a unified perceptual map of the current challenge.

As suggested above, the right hemisphere sensory lobes process the novel—and the left hemisphere sensory lobes process the familiar—elements of a challenge.

The frontal lobes determine an appropriate response strategy. The right hemisphere frontal lobe develops creative solutions to novel challenges, and the left hemisphere frontal lobe activates established routines.

The sensory lobes are more synchronized because it's important to have a unified perception of the environment. The frontal lobes are less synchronized because it's useful to view problems from various perspectives.

We can thus think of the cerebral cortex as a quadrant individually and collaboratively equipped to efficiently recognize (sensory lobes) and respond (frontal lobes) to the novel (right hemisphere) and familiar (left hemisphere) challenges that we confront in the space-time environment we inhabit.

How elegant! And, our brain's 20-year developmental trajectory is equally elegant.

Development
and Growth

From Womb to World

Chapter 3 described how our brain is organized to carry out its functions, but it didn't indicate how our brain's undifferentiated cellular beginnings eventually develop into what is generally considered to be the most complex three pounds of matter in the known universe. So, let's explore human development and growth in this chapter—with a special focus on the prepuberty years.

The terms *development* and *growth* are often used interchangeably, but they're different, and the difference is important when nurturing children. We *observe* development and we *nurture* growth.

Development involves the addition or modification of structures or abilities, and growth involves a measurable increase in an existing condition, such as in size or competence. A tree grows in size, but it develops new branches and roots. Students grow in their competence with addition, but they then develop multiplication skills. A community grows in size and population, but it may develop a new rapid transit system. Development typically leads to growth if we toss energy and nurturing into the mix.

We appropriately modify some forms of growth and development, such as by cutting fingernails and removing warts, but trying to accelerate or delay the maturation of reasonably normal juveniles is problematic. It's probably better to simply observe and nurture. Children tend to provide observant adults with plenty of clues about when they're ready to develop and explore a new concept or skill and also about how far they might want its development to grow. It's therefore inappropriate to try to teach a one-month-old child to walk, and it's also inappropriate to not enhance the mobility skills of a one year old.

GROWTH AND DEVELOPMENT AS REDUCTIVE

Although it seems counterintuitive, development and growth in individuals or in social phenomena often involve a reduction rather than an increase. For example, infants are born capable of speaking all of the languages in the world, but they're not born proficient in any of them. Unless we're reared in a multilingual community, we typically develop proficiency in only one language. We similarly are capable at birth of developing a wide variety of interests, skills, vocational goals, friendships, and the like, but we typically reduce these to a manageable few as we go through life.

Just as the development and ending of contested social phenomena—such as presidential elections and sports seasons—are also unpredictable, the process similarly begins with many entrants and ends with one winner, but the winnowing process itself is typically interesting and useful.

Think of a dandelion. Only a very few of its 2,000-plus seeds will become mature plants, but during the plant's lifespan, they'll all participate in a botanical sequence that provides a piquant leafy addition to spring salads, delights most of us with its summer flowers, and amuses seed-blowing children. Bonus: It also provides wine for people, food for animals, and, eventually, compost for the soil. The plant and seed are oblivious to all of this. It's we observers who are intrigued by the growth and developmental stages and ecological richness of a plant that many consider a weed.

A human sperm cell (which similarly can evoke interest) gets only one very slim opportunity for genetic immortality. Given the terrible odds, testes produce many millions of sperm in each effort, in the continuing optimistic hope that one will connect with a ripe maternal ovum. To further complicate matters, sperm need a host who is sufficiently appealing to attract the interest of the owner of the ovum—and on the right days of the month to boot. And unlike dandelion seeds, sperm don't even get to be blown about in the sunshine for awhile before they succeed or fail. Human sperm may innately hope for an extended productive life, but precious few get it. They do what they can to make their short life exciting for their host, and they let it go at that.

About 400 of the 400,000 immature ova that a girl has in her ovaries at birth mature and are released during her reproductive years. They are the largest cells in her body. Most obviously suffer the same fate as sperm. Like sperm, they are fully prepared to begin an extended productive human life, but only a few, if any, will get it.

This reductive process continues after birth. During most of human history, childhood death was common. It's been only during the last half century that medical advances have significantly reduced childhood deaths caused by genetic disorders, infectious diseases, and accidents.

Perhaps that's why humans still consider survival itself to be significant and, further, to define a successful life in terms of publicly recognized accomplishments rather than to celebrate the simple growth and developmental trajectory itself. The winner of a silver medal in the Olympics may thus feel a sense of defeat at not winning the gold medal—that being the second best in the world somehow signals failure.

It's important to realize that our journey to cognitive maturity takes at least 20 years, and that each child follows a unique trajectory that includes many ups and downs. It's thus normal for children to exhibit limited competence in many areas of life and to constantly shift interests. What they may eventually accomplish isn't currently as important as living each developmental day to its fullest.

I memorized Thomas Gray's "Elegy Written in a Country Churchyard" during my high school years and have always been most impressed by the verse:

Full many a gem of purest ray serene

The dark unfathomed caves of ocean bear:

Full many a flower is born to blush unseen,

And waste its sweetness on the desert air. (Gray, 1955, p. 348)

To believe that a gem's value is dependent on whether humans feature it in crafted jewelry, or that a flower's value is dependent on humans being able to see and smell it, misses the point of the intrinsic value of every living and nonliving thing—at whatever its current level of growth and development, at wherever it currently resides.

A sperm and egg meet, and human growth and development begin. Adults should provide unconditional love and nurturing—to hope for the best but to nurture whatever develops. A child who could initially become *anyone* will become *just one*. The reduction that defines adult life is yet to come. We have one limitless childhood in our lifetime, and it ought to be significant, interesting, and enjoyable in itself.

Prenatal Development

Our brain and skin are the first two organs to emerge in the developing embryo. About two weeks after conception, they begin to develop out of the same layer of embryonic tissue (the **ectoderm**). The cells on one side initiate the development of the eight-pound, 22-square-foot mantle of skin that surrounds our adult body, and the cells on the other side develop into our three-pound adult brain. We can thus think of our skin as the outside layer of our brain, because all of our brain's sensory receptors are embedded in skin or in sense organs that are embedded in skin.

Our fetal brain is about a half-inch long at 10 weeks, and it is two inches at 20 weeks. The cortex that processes conscious thought and action develops during that 10-week period. In describing the organization of the cortex, Chapter 3 reported that the tens of billions of cortical neurons are arranged in six very distinct horizontal layers, but they are also arranged into vertical columns that transverse the six layers, with each column processing a specific cognitive task.

Developing the cortex would thus seem to be a very complicated task, but it does have intriguing functional parallels to the construction of a six-story building—a simple model that an elementary student could understand. The building's girders go up first, and then the floors, walls, and other elements are added—beginning with the first floor and continuing up to the sixth floor.

In our brain, fibers that project from a very large number of glial cells connect what will become the bottom and top of the cortex (think building girders). A similarly large number of **stem cells** that will synthesize the cortical neurons are located at the bottom (think construction materials). The stem cells divide, and the daughter cell from each such division attaches to and climbs up an adjacent glial projection to where the bottom layer of the cortex (layer six) will develop. They then leave their glial projection and the aggregate of the first set of synthesized migrating neurons form the lowest cortical layer (think first floor). The next set of synthesized neurons climbs past the first layer and creates the second layer. The process continues in this manner over the 10-week developmental period until the six-layer cortex (the gray matter) is complete.

The neurons assemble also into vertical columns that transverse the six layers, develop **dendrites** that will receive messages from other neurons, and send out an axon extension into the underlying white matter that will connect the neurons in a column with other cortical columns and brain systems. Think of how the businesses in a building use surface and electronic transmission systems to send and receive messages from businesses in other buildings. Chapter 3 reported that related columns also form into larger integrated systems, such as the various hemispheric lobes and subsystems within a lobe (such as the columns in the motor cortex that regulate movement in the fingers of our right or left hand). Think of specialized areas in a city (such as those that focus on retail, manufacturing, or governmental services) and how these various community systems carry out both individual and collaborative activities.

Postnatal Development

Simply put, our brain develops functional competence from the bottom to the top, from the back to the front, and from the right to the left. To summarize the extensive Chapter 3 description, the **brainstem** at the base of our brain regulates body systems, and so it must be functional at birth. The **cerebrum** at the top develops competency over the 20-year developmental trajectory. The sensory lobes at the back of the cortex that develop principally during childhood recognize and interpret the challenges we confront, and the frontal lobes that mature principally during adolescence develop appropriate responses to such challenges. The novel challenges we confront are processed principally in the right hemisphere's sensory and frontal lobes, and familiar challenges are processed principally in the left hemisphere's sensory and frontal lobes. Childhood is replete with novelty, so a child's right hemisphere is very active.

The birth canal of a mother cat or similar animal is slightly larger than its baby, so a kitten is born with an almost fully developed brain. A feral cat can survive after about three months.

As reported in Chapter 1, humans are born with a very immature brain, about 1/3 the three-pound adult size, because they must be able to emerge from women who walk upright and consequently have narrower birth canals than other animals. We're born with functioning survival systems (such as circulation and respiration), but most other brain systems are only at a level of developmental readiness. Because our brain's principal task is to regulate movement, one would expect this to be the major developmental priority, and it is.

Our brain doubles in weight during its first year, and much of this increase is centered in the **cerebellum**, which coordinates sensory perception and automatic movement programs. The development of motor competence emanates outward from an infant's brain. Head and mouth movements become functional before arm and hand movements, which become functional before leg and foot movements. So, infants can suckle before they can grasp before they can walk. In effect, brain and body connect functionally during our first year.

The third pound of brain develops and grows over the next 19 or so years, and most of that is in the cerebrum. In effect, our child and adolescent body/brain connects with its environment. We learn how the world works and how best to respond to its continuous challenges. We learn how to communicate and socialize with others. We discover who we are and how we relate to the complex world we inhabit.

Our helpless beginning and long juvenile dependency combined to make us a cooperative social species with a rich language-driven culture. Social skills are thus developmentally important, and in our complex society, it's very important that immature children learn how to collaborate effectively with those who aren't kin and with those who don't even share the values and traditions that are important to one's supportive family.

Our brain's early development is focused on genetically driven species-specific processing systems. Later development focuses on environmentally driven culturally specific processing systems. For example, our ability to speak is innate, but learning to speak a specific language is culturally specific.

We're born with a basic, survival-level version of most brain systems, and it functions at that level with limited instruction and effort. Learning how to talk and walk and the startle reflex are examples of innate, easily mastered human capabilities.

Explicit instruction and extended practice mature such systems so that they can respond to more complex culturally driven challenges. Learning how to read or to tap dance are thus learned extensions of talking and walking. Learning how to respond to potential cultural dangers (such as how to cross a street or handle a knife) is similarly a learned extension of the startle reflex.

A normal human ability range exists that limits responses beyond this range to virtuosos and savants, and to the technologies that we develop to extend performance of the function beyond our biological capabilities. The Olympics high-jump competition represents the virtuoso level of human jumping ability without technological support, and the pole vault competition is its technologically augmented analogue. Our ability to talk is innate, but reading must be learned and writing requires an instrument such as a pencil or keyboard. Automobiles are technological extensions of our legs. Freeway medians and stoplights reduce the threat of vehicular danger, and so they extend our innate startle reflex.

Chapter 1 reported that children develop a basic competence in culturally important knowledge and skills and in the technologies that enhance human capability through play, games, and specific instruction. Informal exploration and explicit instruction continue to be important throughout life as we meet and master new challenges.

The First 20 Years. To simplify a complex phenomenon, we can divide our 20-year developmental trajectory into two periods of approximately 10 years each. The developmental period from birth to about age 10 focuses on learning how to be *a human being*—learning to move, to communicate, and to master basic social skills. The developmental period from about 11 to 20 focuses on learning how to be *a productive reproductive human being*—planning for a vocation, exploring emotional commitment and sexuality, and achieving autonomy.

The first four years of each of these two decade-long developmental periods are characterized by slow awkward beginnings prior to a six-year normal move toward confidence and competence. For example, crawling leads to toddling leads to walking leads to running and leaping.

We've designed our preschool, elementary school, middle school, high school, and initial college systems around this rhythmic four-six-four-six-year developmental sequence. We tend to keep small children at home during their first four years to allow them to begin their development in a sheltered family environment without state standards and assessment programs. They learn basic motor skills, how to talk, and how to get along with their families. In essence, they develop a basic understanding of how their sheltered world works.

At about five years, we say, in effect, "You can do it with kin, can you do it with non-kin?" We then put them in a kindergarten classroom with a non-kin teacher and a couple dozen similarly aged children, and this ratchets up the motor, language, cultural, and social knowledge and skills they have to master. For example, learning to read and write are more complex than learning to talk, the factual information they learn extends beyond their homes, and they have to learn how to get along with children who aren't related to them. By the time they reach fifth grade (about age 10) and their sensory lobes are at a reasonable level of maturity, most have learned a lot about how the world works.

The middle school and preschool years are developmentally similar in that they both represent the initial awkward development of important brain systems and cognitive functions: sensory lobe recognition capabilities during the preschool years and frontal lobe response capabilities during the middle school years.

We tend to be far more indulgent of the inevitable developmental awkwardness and errors of young children than of related early adolescent awkwardness and errors. Demanding adults tend to forget that the mastery of something as complex as reflective thought or one's sexuality didn't occur instantly and without error in their lives, and it likewise probably won't in an adolescent's life.

Competence during the first 10 years is characterized by a move toward rapid automatic responses to challenges. For example, slow laborious initial reading tends to become reasonably automatic by age 10.

Language includes the automatic mastery of a verbal taxonomy of generally accepted object, action, quality, and relationship categories. Similarly, morality and ethics include the mastery of a social taxonomy of culturally acceptable behaviors, such as to share and be fair.

Competence during the second 10 years, however, is often appropriately characterized by delayed and reflective responses processed principally in the frontal lobes. For example, the common impulsive, instant-gratification childhood responses become less impulsive as a maturing adolescent learns to explore options and social implications prior to making a response.

In effect, cognitive development during the first 10 years focuses on recognizing and understanding the dynamics of various environmental challenges that are processed principally in the sensory lobes, and cognition during the second 10 years focuses on developing effective and appropriate problem-solving strategies for such challenges as are processed principally in the frontal lobes.

The cultural strategy for dealing with children with immature frontal lobes is to expect the adults in their lives to make many frontal lobe decisions for them—where to live, what to wear, when to go to bed, and so forth. Children with immature frontal lobes are willing to let adults make such decisions. Infants who can't walk are similarly willing to let adults carry them. But, just as young children generally don't want to be carried while they're learning to walk, adolescents don't want adults to make frontal lobe decisions for them while their frontal lobes are maturing.

The only way we can learn to walk is to practice walking, and the only way we can mature our frontal lobes is to practice the reflective problem-solving and advanced social skills that our frontal lobes regulate, even though young people aren't very successful with it initially. Adolescence thus becomes a challenge for both the adolescents and the significant adults in their lives.

Part 2

Nurturing Childhood

Nurturing

From Unconditional
Love to Behavioral Limits

When my wife and I conceived our children, we combined our genetic histories to write the first page in the lives of these new human beings. The many possible combinations of fewer than two-dozen amino acids represented within our combined DNA provided each developing embryo with all the coded genetic information they needed to build their bodies—nose and ear placement, skin and eye color, plus all the other common and unique factors that make a child both a human being and an individual person.

Children are born helpless. Adults must thus shelter and nurture them in a safe and healthy environment during their extended juvenile development, teaching them basic survival, personal, and social skills. Much of the initial postbirth nurturing is communicated through a verbal code that uses the many possible combinations of fewer than four dozen phonemes (in English) to create a complex language. Transforming spoken phonemes into a written alphabet allows slightly older children to learn from people beyond their immediate family and friends, so the childhood mastery of reading is essential to enculturation.

How amazing that two simple, similar codes that function via various sequences of a relatively few amino acids and phonemes/letters can regulate so much of the complexities of human life. As Chapter 1 suggested, the genetic code is focused on how to *become* a human being, and the language code is focused on how to *behave* like a human being.

We develop our behavioral skills during a sheltered childhood and an increasingly independent adolescence, and we activate them as autonomous adults. We typically live within relatively simple family, neighborhood, and classroom environments during childhood and adolescence, but adult life typically inserts us into a large number of more complex social groups. So when children are born or enter an elementary classroom, parents and teachers should accept them for who they are at that developmental moment, but they should also consider how best to nudge the child into the subsequent stages that lead to a successful adult life within the social frameworks that define human life.

BONDING

Biological bonding within the family begins the optimistic process, and cultural bonding within a classroom and community continues it. It's important that children are inherently attracted to and bond with the significant adults in their lives and vice versa; otherwise, they might wander off and no one would care.

Bonding is so important to our survival and the quality of our lives that many neuronal and chemical systems participate in bonding children and their parents and, later, in romantically bonding adult couples who fall in love. For example, the **hypothalamus, caudate nucleus, nucleus accumbens, septum,** and several frontal lobe areas are especially active when we bond and fall in love, and **oxytocin, vasopressin, testosterone, estrogen, endorphin, dopamine, norepinephrine, serotonin,** and **pheromones** are the molecules that activate and inhibit the body/brain systems that regulate the behaviors of bonding and love. Bonding is a big operation.

Oxytocin and the endorphins are especially important examples. Oxytocin initiates the uterine contractions in childbirth and lactation in breast feeding, but it also enhances bonding and social behaviors. Breast feeding is mutually satisfying in that it reduces the pressure in the mother's full breast and adds food to the infant's empty stomach. The nursing embrace in itself increases endorphin levels in both mother and infant. Every feeding thus enhances bonding, as do the related behaviors that occur in bottle feeding and other parent-child cuddling behaviors.

Children soon realize how dependent they are on their parents, and they are typically distressed when their parents aren't near. Parents are similarly distressed when their children wander off.

The mirror neuron system and parent-child togetherness insures that much of a child's initial behavior is a reflection of closely observed parental behavior. In effect, the parental mind and behavior become the child's initial mind and behavior. Both typically like what they observe in each other, and the result is that parents' unconditional love of their infant tends to emerge effortlessly.

Unconditional love is to love others for who they are, rather than for how they behave. Conditional love is the reward a child gets for doing what a parent requests. It establishes the bonding relationship as something that's dependent on satisfying parental desires, rather than on developing one's personal interests and collaborative skills in a mutually accepting bonded relationship.

Siblings, grandparents, and other relatives and friends become the extended family who also lavish unconditional love and attention on an infant. The child's just being an infant is enough for them. So, life typically begins with a lot of unconditional love, as infants bring just themselves and no initial conscious misbehavior to their birth. Misbehavior that may affect their relationships will occur over time, however.

Bonding and the Teacher. I suspect, on the basis of a long career in education, that the biological systems that enhance parent-child bonding are also operative at some level in many teacher-student relationships. A few such relationships in just about every elementary class become psychologically close, and a few remain distant. It's possible though for teachers to at least develop a feeling of unconditional respect (if not genuine love) for the entire class, just as parents can unconditionally love all their children. Teachers learn early in their careers that classroom life will be difficult if they don't unconditionally respect all their students and encourage the same level of unconditional respect within the class.

Teaching allows a person who enjoys working with children to select and work for years with a compatible age group. Teachers whose own children are grown can continue to work with children, and those who like children but have none of their own can teach them. It's thus a wonderfully fulfilling career for many.

Teachers choose to become teachers. Those who enter teaching know what they're getting into because almost everyone spends at least 12 formative years in classrooms. It's a demanding profession, and so it's difficult to imagine people selecting it if they don't enjoy interacting with a couple dozen children for several hours a day.

This is truer now than several decades ago, when many women who really wanted to enter such vocations as business, law, or medicine became teachers as an alternate choice because their first choice had artificial employment barriers, many of which have now appropriately fallen.

My optimistic view of bonding is obviously not foolproof. It's possible for a parent or child to have a minimally functioning bonding system, and it's possible for someone to become a teacher for reasons other than a desire to work with children. I do believe, however, that the overwhelming majority of both parents and teachers begin with the best of intentions, and that they hope for the best for their charges. Our society fortunately has backup systems (such as schools, social service agencies, and religious organizations) that can both supplement and supplant families with child-parent problems.

Many children tend at least initially to view parents, teachers, and other significant adults in their lives in heroic terms. Children often confront problems they can't resolve—from a dirty diaper in infancy to a dirty epithet at school—so adults who can gracefully solve such problems tend to impress them. They also obviously learn much by observing how their *heroes* solve such problems and how they move effectively through life's daily challenges. Bonding is thus enhanced when the adults are effective role models.

This heroic perspective diminishes during adolescence, when adolescents begin to compare their parents and teachers with others they meet, and they realize that their adult life won't be spent with their childhood family and friends. It's thus probably a good idea for adolescents and their parents to temporarily weaken existing bonds so the adolescents can expand their perspectives, and that typically occurs. It's not a negative development, but rather an essential step toward adult autonomy. If we can successfully bond with our parents and other adults when we're young, we can repeat the process with others during adult life and then also establish an appropriate adult relationship with our parents. Imagine life if we couldn't shift from our initial bonding relationships.

REGULATING

A major childhood developmental task is to understand how the world works. If I drop something, will it bounce, break, or splat? Children learn much of this by directly interacting with the environment, and parents, school, and mass media teach them the things that exist beyond their immediate environment or that aren't immediately apparent, such as how to spell *bounce, break,* and *splat.* Children master some things with relative ease and others with difficulty.

When children begin to develop their cognitive and motor systems, they confront the central concept of biological range. How far can they reach and throw, run and jump? How far can they memorize the multiplication tables? They also confront the range of cultural appropriateness in behavior. Is it better to ask for or to take a toy from a sibling? Childhood is thus focused on discovering what's biologically possible and culturally appropriate and on becoming comfortable within such ranges. Much of what we call *childhood misbehavior* is a result of children's explorations into potentially dangerous and uncomfortable situations near or beyond the limits of a range.

It's important to realize, however, that such explorations at the edges aren't necessarily bad, as they can also lead to virtuosity, creativity, and invention. The adults in their lives must thus walk a fine line between encouraging exploration and discouraging exploitation within the biologically possible and culturally appropriate ranges that children inhabit.

Biologically Possible. We're biologically excellent, but not perfect. The biological costs in terms of our body/brain capabilities would be enormous if we could live for centuries rather than decades, if we didn't have to worry about infections or malignancies, and if we had limitless sensorimotor ranges. We thus have many limitations, but we also have exceptional frontal lobe capabilities that allow us to technologically go beyond the range of our biological limitations. The result is that we now tend to live longer than our ancestors, can cure many debilitating illnesses, and have extended our sensorimotor range with such technologies as microscopes and telescopes, automobiles and airplanes.

It's also important to our survival that we're a social species, with a human capability range in any area that is broader than the range of the typical individual. This led to the wonderful concept of a division of labor that allows people like me with a very narrow capability range in car repair to hire the brains and brawn of those who are much more capable—and for university students to hire folks like me.

Children confront the concept of biological range as they move from grasping to throwing, from crawling to running. Our capability range typically expands fast and far when we're young, and diminishes to slow and close when we're old. We've discovered most of our limitations by the time we reach adulthood, and we typically adapt our lives to them. Young children need supervision because their exploratory curiosity is frequently greater than their motor capabilities, as well as their sense of limitations and danger. Chapter 2 reported the strong desire that children have to explore and master their personal and technologically enhanced movements, and how play and games provide the principal venue for mastery.

Adults initially help children as they learn how to handle objects and move about. Throughout life, we appreciate help when we need it but not when we don't. So, even though children appreciate guiding arms during their first faltering steps, they intuitively know that they'll never learn to walk independently if we continue to help them when they've moved beyond toddling. "I can do it by myself" becomes a childhood mantra. They'll tumble now and again, and may cry because of it, but when children are developing their motor and other cognitive skills, they mostly need adults who are nearby, observant, and supportive but not overprotective.

As children begin to master a skill, we should engage them in play and game activities that will enhance the skill. Children learn from observing our movements (think mirror neurons), but they also learn from observing how we respect our own biological limits and the rights of others who are affected by our behavior.

When children get frustrated at their lack of success, it's often best to simply suggest switching to another activity that they can handle better and come back later to practice the frustrating task. Skills become automatic when mastered, so the combination of conversation and practice during play and games helps children to shift the skill's regulation from a conscious to an automatic level.

We've seen a shift in recent decades from informal games that children organized and managed themselves to highly organized leagues with uniforms, adult coaches, schedules, trips, and parents shouting from the sidelines. While many consider this shift regrettable, such formal programs can be helpful for many children if the supervising adults consider motor skill and social development to be more important than team wins. It can further be helpful for children to work with coaches who don't have the close emotional attachment of a parent and so view a child's successes and failures from a more objective perspective.

This of course is what occurs when children go to school. They have an opportunity to continually compare their motor and intellectual development with a couple dozen non-kin classmates. They typically don't have the same need to emotionally please their teacher that they have with their parents, and they soon realize that their classmates exhibit a range of ability in almost everything—that each student is good in some things and not so good in others. That's something they can't experience as well at home. Teachers should thus view a class as a group of students who are following varying trajectories on a developmental trip. State standards and assessment programs may make this difficult, but it's important to reduce the performance pressure on students as much as possible.

It comes down to this: Parents should observe their child carefully to identify and encourage interests and strengths and to create an accepting home environment that patiently shores up weaknesses. Teachers work with a room full of children, and so they should provide students with many opportunities to self-select activities and thus develop their capabilities in areas that interest them. Self-selection is also operative in informal neighborhood play. Children informally assess each other, and their mirror neuron systems help them move toward the skill level of other more competent friends.

What shouldn't occur is that the push to mastery gets out of hand. For example, we appreciate the virtuoso skills exhibited by young gymnasts in the Olympic Games and other competitions, but I suspect that most of us also have this gnawing voyeuristic feeling that we're observing possible negative effects on the athletes' immature bodies as they practice and perform increasingly complicated and difficult routines. Further, we think about the effect on their childhoods as they devote extended time to intense high-stakes practice that most children devote to informal play. The location of the line between helping children reach their potential in something that really interests them and child abuse isn't clear, but it's a concern that parents and adults who work with children must continually contemplate. Is what's occurring a response to the child's genuine interest and talent, or is it a response to my remembered childhood or current adult fantasy?

Problems will arise. Children don't have the mature frontal lobe capabilities that sound judgment requires, so the adults in their lives in effect become their frontal lobes. Because mature frontal lobes warn us that a proposed behavior is unwise and provide the reason for it, it's appropriate for adults who have the judgment that children lack to stop the inappropriate behavior of children, but they should also explain why: "No, you can't do that because it's dangerous." "You can't do it now, but you can do it when you know how to do it correctly and safely, and I'll help you to learn that." "No, you can't do it that way because it's dangerous, but I'll show you how to use this much safer tool."

Culturally Appropriate. Children soon discover what they can and can't do biologically, but knowing whether a behavior is culturally appropriate is more complicated. Children are born into already existing cultural conventions and family rules and rituals. Their immature brains can't immediately fathom the reason for any of these, so they tend to accept them at face value.

A child's needs are typically personal and immediate, and societal needs are more focused on group values and long-term goals. That disconnect is probably where much misbehavior emerges. How does one explain something as abstract as delayed gratification and cultural values to a loudly insistent child?

What we thus tend to do initially with young children is to operate at the level of directives, which unfortunately often include threats and punishment. The long-term success of such directives (and consequent diminishing of threats and punishments) will depend on our own behavior. If we explain the directives and model the behavior we expect of children, they're much more apt to view our directives as being tuned into the way the world works and to behave appropriately.

For example, children who biologically need 10 hours of sleep at night should go to bed at 9:00 p.m. if they must get up by 7:00 a.m. to go to school. Even first graders can do the math on something like that. If they want to stay up a half hour later to see a TV show, offer to tape it and play it after they come home from school the next day. If they frequently beg for a few more minutes to finish a video game or some other activity, regularly remind them of the time a half hour before they should go to bed. Approaching such issues in a reasonable manner communicates to them that such directives aren't arbitrary.

Similarly, if we expect children to keep their rooms clean, pick up after themselves, and complete assigned chores, we should do the same.

Natural Consequences and Fairness. In addition to helping us compare our biological capabilities, games help teach children the concept of culturally appropriate behavior. Games require cooperation among competitors with opposing goals. Many game rules are arbitrary, but the players agree to abide by them, and (in some games) to a referee's adjudication of disagreements. Two central concepts in life and games that relate to developing culturally appropriate behavior are *natural consequences* and *fairness.*

Games help children to comprehend the important concept of natural consequences—the decisions that we make will positively or negatively affect what occurs next. If we overturn a glass of water, we'll have to clean up the mess. A player who doesn't consider what his opponent in a board game might do may lose a piece or position. Getting angry or crying at our bad fortune won't change the situation. We made an error, and we have to deal with the consequences. Playing games with children thus gives adults a wonderful opportunity to help them compare the realities of games and life. Although cultural and game rules may be arbitrary, folks have agreed to them. We may not benefit from a rule in a given instance, but the worse option is to play without rules. For example, there's no inherent logic in cars driving on either the right or left side of the street, but there's a lot of logic in everyone in a country agreeing to drive the same way.

Because rules are arbitrary, they can be changed prior to the game if need be. Golfers use the concept of a handicap to make the match more competitive. I recall a related childhood arrangement we had in our neighborhood softball games that gave younger players four strikes. It wasn't altruism. We needed enough players to play the game, and so we figured out something to encourage younger children to play with us and so to develop the skills that would make future games more interesting. This suggests that although children may lack adult judgment, they can effectively participate in the development and adaptation of many family and classroom behavioral rules. It was always a big deal for a younger player to graduate from four to three strikes.

Four strikes seemed fair to us, and *fairness* is a deeply ingrained concept that's central to appropriate behavior. Fairness requires a memory that can store and recall prior experiences and especially reciprocal behaviors. An innate (principally) frontal lobe system that matures through experience processes the key strategy for regulating reciprocity, a strategy commonly called tit-for-tat: Cooperate with others on the first encounter, and then imitate whatever the other person does on subsequent occasions (or to modify the Biblical injunction, *Do unto others as they have done unto you*). We see this at many levels, such as in reciprocated Christmas card mailings that continue until one person drops the other, and in our tendency to quit patronizing a business that gave poor value but to give it another chance with a change in ownership.

Young children typically begin to develop tit-for-tat beliefs and behaviors, and the ability to detect cheating in others, through informal play with family and friends and by carrying out household tasks imposed by their parents. School provides a more complicated formal setting that introduces them to (1) a large non-kin group in a limited enclosed space and (2) deferred rewards and punishments, such as within extended curricular projects and grades based on weeks of cumulated work.

Our emotional body language is somewhat transparent, so we become adept at detecting the subtle guilt signals that tit-for-tat cheaters often send. We similarly exhibit emotional displays that express our feelings to others about exchanges (for example, gratitude suggests fairness, and anger suggests unfairness). We tend to break off relationships that become untrustworthy.

Such experiences eventually move us toward a selection of personal friendships and business alliances with those we've come to trust. When a relationship reaches a sufficient level of trust through many successful tit-for-tat experiences, the parties often quit *keeping score* and (formally or informally) commit to an extended more-relaxed altruistic relationship. Marriage, family, and collegial partnerships are examples of positive situations in which both parties can assume fair cooperative behavior and trust over an extended period. The emergence of democratic societies certainly demonstrates a deeply felt need for fairness in government, but we also see it in the long-term success of businesses and other social organizations that function in a fair and cooperative manner.

Our complex society also requires a more abstract altruistic commitment: to do things for others with no hope of return (such as donating money to charitable organizations that will probably never help us). Further, we normally tip selected service employees (such as waiters), although we could usu-ally get away without leaving a tip. Children need to begin to add these kinds of behaviors to their repertoire of culturally appropriate behaviors.

Our sense of fairness begins to develop during childhood. Children rank teacher fairness as a very important quality in studies that have been done of students' attitudes about teacher behavior. Further, experienced educators know that teachers viewed as unfair by their students tend to experience a lot of tit-for-tat student misbehavior—*do unto others as they have done unto you.*

It's in the best interest of adults who work with children to maintain a positive relationship with them. Parental bonds and respect for teachers can weaken if children feel that they're being mistreated. Adults should thus communicate that they are in control but not controlling and that they are willing to collaborate with children to solve problems.

Still, we all have a right to a safe environment, and so adults should intervene decisively when children's inappro-priate behavior portends danger to themselves and others. Hitting a child simply tends to make a bad situation worse. A *time out* is a commonly used strategy that separates the child and others from a potentially worse situation, or that provides an opportunity for the child to contemplate and rectify the sit-uation that developed, or that simply allows the child to ben-efit from a temporary change of venue. Adults should explain why they're providing a time out when they impose it, but they should also explain that adults also have time outs for basically the same reasons. We call them prisons, marriage retreats, and vacations.

Think also of *time in* for children who don't need to con-template as much as they need to activate. A few minutes of jump rope, dance, or other exercise will activate their brains, given that our brain's principal task is to regulate movement. And like with *time out*, it's important for adults to explain the purpose of *time in*. It helps them to *burn off energy* that they're currently spending in negative thoughts and behavior. It also activates our attentional system and reduces stress. It's basically a positive way to reduce a negative situation, and it teaches a strategy that they can use when they feel antsy or when they're close to a fight. Use time in to turn a potential fight into a much more pleasant game in which they have to collaborate, such as riding a teeter totter, playing catch, or moving objects from here to there in a wagon.

Pain helps to identify the nature and location of a body problem, and misbehavior helps to identify the nature and location of an interpersonal problem. Pain and misbehavior are thus diagnostic, and so they are not necessarily negative. Thinking in diagnostic rather than punitive terms communicates a sense of unconditional love, and providing unconditional love to a child passes it forward into the next generation.

Family and Friends

From Close to Loose Bonds

We're born into our family's nested confines, and we typically begin our migrations beyond home during late adolescence. The in-between years allow us to understand and embrace our family's values and dynamics, and to make initial steps toward personal and social identity. One potential problem is that many young parents are in the beginning stages of developing their family's values. They may thus disagree on central parenting issues and so send mixed messages to their child.

It's not necessarily a serious problem. Chapter 5 suggested that the unconditional love implicit in bonding works both ways. The parents accept their child's messes and crying, and the child accepts inconsistent parenting. With luck and mutual acceptance, they'll all improve over time.

Because parents control the early trips beyond the nest, such as neighborhood play, school choice, and community programs, they tend to select venues and experiences that support their own emerging or developed values. For example, most parents involve their children in experiences that they themselves enjoy, such as camping, fishing, visiting museums, and attending religious services.

Children are curious about what their parents do when they *go to work*. Children whose parents farm or run a small business tend to develop a good sense of their parents' vocation because they typically participate in it at some level. The 10-year-old son of the man who fixed our deck last week helped his father. His father pays him, and he told me that he enjoys doing it during summer vacation because he and an older sister each work only two days a week. It was interesting to observe the positive apprenticeship relationship between father and son—to realize that the boy was getting more than spending money for his assistance. A woman who grew up on a farm recently told me that the question never came up about whether she would participate in farm chores. It was simply something she and her siblings did, and although she hasn't spent her adult life on a farm, she feels that she has a good sense of what her parents did and what farming entails.

Conversely, many children today have a limited sense of their parents' vocations, as an increasing number of occupations have shifted from actually producing or repairing something to doing something that's an abstraction to a child. A child can much more easily comprehend what a *carpenter* or *car mechanic* does than a *customer service agent* or *computer systems manager*.

Chapter 5 described the biological and cultural ranges within which children begin the process of comparing how their families and the rest of the world functions. Let's continue that discussion.

CHILDHOOD PLAY

Children must get beyond the bonding focus of family life into the social skills focus of non-kin life. Non-kin life encompasses a lot of strangers and acquaintances and a relatively small number who fit into the category of *friend*. Much of the initial childhood exploration about how the social world works occurs in play and game experiences with other children.

Children vary in how this occurs. Some begin informally with neighborhood children, and some do it through formal play dates that their parents schedule. Our children eased into the process mostly on their own because we lived in a neighborhood with many similar-age children. I can understand, however, that a more structured arrangement is better for many families and neighborhoods. However structured or unstructured the arrangement, children typically spend considerable time in the homes of their friends, and that's where they begin the process of comparing how different families function and of discovering that alternate approaches to family life can be successful.

We're a social species, so the early informal development of basic social skills in nonfamily settings is important. Chapter 5 ended with a discussion of *fairness*, a central element of appropriate social behavior. Other elements that develop during informal childhood activities are the willingness and ability to share, collaborate, and converse. Let's examine them.

Sharing, Collaborating, Conversing. Childhood play often involves objects or equipment that become the focus of the activity. Taking turns thus becomes important, because children are more interested in using the object or equipment than in observing others use it. Throwing a ball back and forth and being on a teeter-totter are examples of shared experiences. Playing with a doll and riding a tricycle are examples of activities in which sharing is a positive but optional element.

Encourage children who are getting acquainted to engage in activities in which sharing is built into the activity, and then use the pleasure that the children get from that shared experience to encourage sharing in activities in which it's optional. This requires children to negotiate such issues as *how long* or *how many times* constitutes a fair turn. It sounds trivial, but this is actually an important concept throughout life. Think about the problems that parents have if they don't equitably share various childrearing and household tasks or family resources.

Collaboration is a more complex element of social learning. It involves a task that a single person can't do easily or at all, and so it requires negotiated responsibilities and procedures. Children tend to get introduced to collaboration in play and games. This has historically occurred via such activities as building Lego structures, creating playhouse environments, and determining the skippers and holders in jump rope, but collaborative electronic games designed for young children have become increasingly popular. Simple introductory activities can lead to more complex collaborations, such as those in team sports and collaborative video games. Here again, the parental and teacher modeling of collaborative behaviors in the real world communicates to children that collaboration is a win-win arrangement. Collaborative play and games also obviously enhance mirror neuron and problem-solving systems.

Collaboration obviously requires communication, and so the development of language skills is enhanced through the explaining and discussing that occurs during sharing and collaborative tasks. Children have to clearly state their desires and intentions, and they must infer those of their playmates. Once again, electronic forms of communication, such as cell phones and text messaging, are changing the nature of social interaction. Most 21st-century children are "bilingual"—in human and electronic languages. For example, text messaging has its own form of spelling and syntax.

In such collaborative activities, observant adults should respond more to the persistent efforts that children make to solve the problem than to the outcome. This kind of process-oriented response encourages children to attempt more difficult challenges, and it reduces any discouragement that failure might bring. To a group of children, we should thus say such things as, "I thought that it was a good idea for you to talk about who should do each part of the activity." And,

"I like the way you talked about how you couldn't put the pieces together and decided to start over again." And, "It was good that the entire class made suggestions and that we tried out those that seemed best before deciding what to do."

It's perhaps important to note here that we share our collaborative drive with much of the biological world, such as the 12,000 species of social insects that have evolved into very complex collaborative communities. We humans are different in that much of our culturally collaborative behavior is learned and not innate.

SCHOOL AND CITIZENSHIP

For most children, school is the major venue for the shift from the informal confines of home and neighborhood to the more formal social complexities of the larger institutionalized world. Young people spend about 1,000 hours a year in school for at least twelve years. They'll be with some classmates and staff members for years. Others will leave and/or arrive within the school year. School thus introduces children to the complexities of dealing with institutions and to a diverse and often transitory population. How can schools in a democratic society best prepare children for their social and civic responsibilities?

Authoritarian governments dominated much of human history. The representative form of democracy initiated in the United States was a bold political experiment in collaborative governance that has taken 200-plus years to develop, and it is still continuously evolving through challenges by individuals, groups, and events. Our democratic society is characterized as much by disagreement as by agreement, but we've learned over the years how to disagree without being unduly disagreeable. In our democracy, the majority vote settles the disagreement, but the minority can seek redress through the courts and subsequent votes. Individual thought and expression are constitutionally protected, and governments change by vote rather than force.

The rest of the world observed as we gradually worked out the kinks in the system, and an increasing number liked what they observed. About a dozen other democracies had emerged by the beginning of the 20th century, and today, 120 of the 200 or so countries in the world have some form of democratic government. The movement toward democratic forms of government will certainly increase as ease of travel and electronic communication combine to turn the world into even more of a democratically collaborative global village than it currently is.

The philosopher John Dewey (1916) argued eloquently a century ago that maturing citizens in a democratic society deserve a democratically run school. His beliefs seemed reasonable to many, but the Progressive Education Movement he proposed had all but died by the time I began school in the 1930s. Classroom management was viewed as an administrative function—the adults managed the students without student input. The prevailing view was that while our democratic society needed intelligent autonomous citizens, it also needed a compliant workforce who would show up on time and do what the employers asked them to do. The school seemed a good place to teach that. We thus maintained an authoritarian school within a democratic society despite the apparent contradiction.

The serious shift toward democratic schools occurred gradually during the second half of the 20th century. Educators began to realize that classroom management could be viewed as a curricular rather than an administrative function. The classroom could become a social laboratory in which students would collaborate on many of the mundane-to-important decisions that teachers typically make, and they could develop important problem-solving and negotiation skills in the process. School is the only institution in our society in which young folks interact for 13 years with many hundreds of non-kin at a similar developmental stage. What are the options if our society doesn't explicitly develop social and democratic skills within its schools?

A 20th-century society focused on making and moving objects within natural space and time is shifting to a 21st-century society focused on creating and moving information within cyber space and time. This suggests that collaborative and creative behavior may now become as valued as individual and compliant behavior. A democratic school encourages an independent entrepreneurial spirit. In an era in which manufacturing is increasingly outsourced, the development of creative, collaborative, and entrepreneurial abilities becomes critical to our nation's economic future.

Democratic Classrooms

Innovative schools began to explore collaborative classroom-management possibilities several decades ago. The literature that emerged on proposed democratic procedures was and remains intriguingly diverse, but what else would one expect within a democracy replete with differing perspectives about what democracy should be? For example, the two principal U.S. political parties differ considerably in their beliefs on many issues, and substantive differences also exist within each political party.

Collaboration is a central social concept, so it ought also to become central in classroom management (Sylwester, 2003). A democratic classroom-management model doesn't abrogate educators from responsibility. We're a representative democracy, and educators represent society in its desire to maintain a safe, effective learning environment. Individuals in a democracy aren't free to do anything they want. Freedom isn't license. Still, the entire class can democratically make many classroom decisions that teachers now make—if we would put our mind to it. Individual teachers discover that when they make all the management decisions, they are worn out by the end of the day, and their students are bored.

A democratic management model won't solve all the misbehavior problems that students and educators commit. Misbehavior occurs within all management models, and our representative democracy functions effectively with all sorts of misbehavior. For example, Chapter 5 suggested that democracies have an adult version of *time out* called prison. Most individuals and governments are behaviorally excellent but not perfect.

Chapter 5 also suggested that, just as pain is useful in that it identifies the nature and location of a biological problem, misbehavior can be useful when it signals that something isn't functioning as it should. It's a problem to be solved, and it's typically best solved with the collaboration of those who are misbehaving.

Democratic procedures work, despite a constant messy pattern of disagreement and inefficiency, because a democracy is tuned to the striking similarities that biological and social systems exhibit. Managing a country or classroom is functionally similar to body/brain management. We're biased toward challenge—most of our emotions are negative, and much of our cognitive energy is focused on solving problems. When things are running smoothly, we tend to go looking for trouble at both the personal and political level.

We've not discovered a magic formula for creating a democracy in 200-plus years at either the national or classroom level. Developing a perfect formula misses the whole point of the enterprise. A democracy is an unfinished process replete with dangers and opportunities, and our social nature prefers a continuing collaborative search for the solutions. Our nation began with a determination to succeed as a democracy, and then its citizens worked collaboratively to temporarily solve each successive challenge it confronted. Every constitutional amendment and legislative act represents something that wasn't previously right.

Teachers should similarly begin their shift to a truly democratic classroom with honest collaborations that solve simple issues that arise and go on from there. City governments similarly have to fix street potholes as well as solve complex transportation issues.

Think of all the decisions related to classroom space, time, and movement such as furniture arrangement, class schedules, and student movement patterns. Think of all the decisions related to who gets to make the decision and how much energy should be expended on the project. Think of all the decisions related to what's possible and what's appropriate. Students who are encouraged to collaborate in these simple classroom decisions will mature into adults who can collaborate on analogous civic decisions.

Two important questions that students and citizens should continually ask are, Why are we doing this? and Why are we doing it this way and not that way? The questions tend to irritate those in power, but they're central to a democratic society (and classroom). For example, the United States has engaged in two wars during the past 50 years in which the common retrospective view is that we didn't sufficiently attend to the criticisms that occurred prior to the decision. By encouraging these kinds of hard questions on relatively easy classroom problems during the elementary school years, we'll develop citizens who will feel confident to ask them of politicians and others during their adult life.

Begin the year with the simple identification and discussion of the expectations of your students, their parents, and state standards. Encourage students to ask the two *why* questions mentioned above. Move the discussion to things they think might make it difficult to meet the expectations of the three groups. Select one problem with a good probability for a relatively rapid resolution, and collaboratively explore possible solutions. Try the best suggestion, and adapt it if necessary. When you've been at least moderately successful with that problem, select another one and repeat the process. You don't have to collaboratively solve all the problems you and your class confront, because the principal purpose of this exercise is to develop social problem solving skills, not perfect solutions.

A class group may thus not be genuinely democratic in September when they begin their collaborative explorations, but they could be close to it by June if you and your class determine to do it.

The Role of Smiles and Frowns

As children move from home into more complex social settings, such as a school, they need to master positive and negative social signals, especially nonverbal signals. When asked to list qualities they want in a teacher (and other adults, for all that), students tend to give high ratings to a sense of humor, but they typically find it difficult to define it. It seems a matter of recognizing something we experience without being able to precisely define it. Humor is thus a complex social concept with a fuzzy definition, and it's much more than simply the ability to tell jokes.

A sense of humor is a manifestation of the ability to pleasantly signal that current behavior is approaching the edge of what's considered normal and/or acceptable. Young people frequently push at the edges of what's possible and appropriate, because they'll never truly understand normality if they don't discover where it ends (the Olympics being an example of our periodic formal search for selected physical limits). And because young people often lack the experience and maturity of self-assessment, they expect others to help let them know when they've gone too far—albeit with *a sense of humor.*

Think of a behavioral continuum that ranges from abnormally negative to abnormally positive. We all need to know how others view our behavior along this continuum. As our behavior moves toward and into the abnormally negative, others typically let us know with an escalating sequence of responses from simple frowns to outbursts of anger, disgust, and alarm. At the positive end, the sequence shifts from smiles and gentle encouragement to effuse joy and praise.

As suggested above, we could thus view an important much-appreciated element of an adult's sense of humor as being a pleasant, nonthreatening technique for letting children know that they're moving toward *the edge.* The adult inserts an appreciated noncritical smile prior to a frown—intonation and body language communicating that everything's OK for now, but I'm watching you. This gives the child a chance to consider whether to proceed.

Children also appreciate the verbal and body language that communicates the adult's early awareness of behavior that's just beginning to move toward the positive edge of the continuum. It's an initial but escalating encouragement to go further, beyond the normal range. Its smile communicates, "I know you can do it; go for it!"

The term *kidding* is often positively associated with a sense of humor. Sarcasm isn't. To be effective, the indirect language and intonation of kidding must imply a genuine love of and respect for the person being kidded, even though the actual words may suggest negative connotations.

Young children often can't correctly interpret kidding. Our right frontal lobes appear to process the verbal and affective discrepancies that play an important role in humor (and thus in kidding). The immature frontal lobes of young children can't process subtle categorical discrepancies (such as in the puns and word play of kidding). They tend rather to enjoy the humor of broad discrepancies (such as in slapstick humor). Adults thus tend to be direct when advising young children and more indirect with adolescents.

Humor often results in laughter, an ill-understood, instinctive, contagious emotional outburst that can both bond and humiliate people. Positive laughter has the potential to enhance both the health of individuals and group cohesion. In effect, it communicates, "We all understand what's occurring, and it's at *the exciting edge.*" It's thus not surprising that children intuitively appreciate adults with the sense of humor that creates a joyful, nonthreatening situation that's often encroaching upon the edge. The students perhaps can't precisely define the concept, but they certainly do appreciate its ability to reduce the negative feelings of anxiety and stress they would otherwise experience.

So relax and observe your students move toward the positive and negative edges with a genuine smile on your face!

Nutrition

From Necessary to Nice

W e're basically a 27-foot-long mouth-to-anus tube with a body wrapped around it. Our digestive system absorbs nutrients from the food that we insert into the top of the tube, and we excrete whatever our body can't use. It's a simple functional system, but it has complex cultural accompaniments.

We devote much of our time and energy to the acquisition and preparation of food. It's thus not surprising that eating—the activity at the top of the tube—is typically social, celebratory, and replete with rich and pleasant sensory overtones. For example, inserting food into our digestive tube is integral to most gatherings of family and friends, but we also go to restaurants where we shamelessly ingest food in front of strangers. Couples seeking information about each other often incorporate eating into their initial meetings. We read magazines and books devoted to the preparation and presentation of food. Some foods, such as pizzas, birthday cakes, and Thanksgiving turkeys are almost communal by definition. Similarly, potlucks, cafeterias, and food sharing in Asian restaurants are examples of communal eating arrangements. *Communion* is a key element of many Christian church services—services that are often followed by coffee, cookies, and conversation in the parish hall.

The inevitable conclusion of the movement of food through our digestive tubes is anything but social and cele-bratory, let alone romantic and replete with pleasant sensory overtones. It's private, and much of it is incorporated into our shame culture. We teach children euphemisms for the more descriptive terms, but then use the descriptive terms to express disgust and to defame others. Further, defecation cer-tainly doesn't have an equivalent to the top-of-the-tube con-cept of *gourmet*. It's also odd that all family members easily share home toilet facilities, but we separate males and females in public facilities.

This *social-input–private-output* arrangement also occurs in related activities. For example, shopping for groceries in busy attractive stores is often a social, celebratory event, but several nights later we'll privately push the garbage and recycling containers out to the curb for pickup the next day by the local refuse company.

Family Food Patterns

Chapter 6 began with the comment that we're born into our family's nested confines, and we typically begin our extended migrations during late adolescence. The childhood years are thus principally about learning and embracing our family's values and dynamics and making initial steps toward per-sonal and social identity. One potential problem is that young parents may still be so closely tied to their own family's tradi-tions that they find it difficult to create a new blended family identity on such issues as food preferences and eating pat-terns. In addition, allergies and religious beliefs can affect how individuals and families approach eating and nutrition. Such parental differences can confuse children.

It's not necessarily a serious problem. Chapter 5 suggested that the unconditional love implicit in bonding works both ways. The parents accept their child's food aversions and eating misbehavior, and the child accepts inconsistent and confusing parenting. With luck and mutual acceptance, they'll all improve over time.

It's important for a family to eat together, even though it's often difficult to arrange it. Family meals help to develop a cohesive, healthier family, given that a prepared meal is less apt to be composed of fast-food convenience and junk-food nutrition.

Because eating has important cultural overtones, children must learn appropriate behavior, and this is best learned through the regular observation of parental and sibling behavior. Family meals also provide a good opportunity for informal family conversation, and conversation is integral to much of the eating that we do throughout life. My wife and I decided from the beginning to eat dinner as a family, and so we all shared our day's experiences, told jokes, disagreed with each other, and solved the world's problems. It persisted. Decades later, the daily family conversation continues, except now it's a vibrant e-mail conversation that connects a geographically separated family—and now the older grandchildren are joining in.

School lunch programs provide another venue for learning appropriate social behavior and for eating foods not commonly prepared at home. School lunch programs are becoming more nutritionally sound, and the cooks often imaginatively prepare appealing versions of foods that many children don't like. The school lunch period shouldn't be a rushed affair, although unfortunately it often is.

NUTRITION

As indicated earlier, our brain encompasses only 2% of our body's weight, but it uses 20% of all our nutrient energy. When we're very active, our brain uses almost as much oxygen as all our muscles combined. When we think about nutrition, we're thus thinking first about our brain's needs.

Our brain is made up of the same materials as our body, so its nutrient needs are similar. Glucose is central to neuronal processing, and amino acids are necessary to **neurotransmitter** synthesis. Blood that is rich in oxygen and nutrients leaves our heart via the aorta, flows into our head via the carotid artery, and then travels throughout our body. Our brain is thus first in line for nutritional support—and it certainly fills its plate.

The blood-brain barrier is a protective layer surrounding our brain's blood vessels (and especially the capillaries). It allows useful materials to pass from the circulatory system into our brain, but it prevents most potentially dangerous materials from entering into brain tissue.

Diet. A reasonably wholesome, balanced diet will take care of our brain's nutrient needs, although the rest of our body (which gets the leavings) may not do as well. The dilemma is to know for sure what a wholesome, balanced diet is, given the variety of current perspectives on diet. But even with all the dietary disagreement, children with a developing brain/body should avoid what are commonly called junk foods and carbonated beverages, and explore the wide range of foods commonly known to be wholesome. Go light on sugar, salt, and fat. Go for a variety of whole grains, vegetables, eggs, dairy products, nuts, and fruits. Think of meat as you think of herbs and spices—a little bit goes a long way. Avoid packaged foods that have a long list of incomprehensible ingredients. Encourage children to drink plain water.

The Electronic Resources section of this book will link you to several excellent websites that provide parents and teachers with very useful current information on childhood nutrition.

Also, the elementary curriculum should play an important supportive role in teaching children about nutrition. Schools can provide useful information in an instructional setting that differs from sitting at a table and actually eating. The information is typically presented more abstractly in a classroom—as words, pictures, and relationships—but children benefit from both kinds of instruction.

PREFERENCES AND AVERSIONS

Parents often wonder why their children refuse to eat some vegetables that most adults like. The answer is intriguing, something that teachers can also explore with their students.

Animals have legs, wings, or fins that allow them to seek food and escape predators. Conversely, immobile plants have roots that anchor them to one location. Their survival thus depends on leaves and roots that absorb the available sunlight, water, and nutrients they need and on biological strategies that discourage the predatory nibbling of herbivores.

Herbivores provide some beneficial services for plants, such as when they eat the fruit that encapsulates a seed and then later excrete the seed at a distance where it can more easily germinate. To protect themselves from destructive nibbling, plants have had to develop defenses, such as bark and hard coverings around fruit or by producing an excess of what the animals eat so that enough remains to maintain the plant.

Perhaps the most intriguing plant defense is one that helps to explain why children often avoid vegetables that they later enjoy as adults. Many plants (and especially wild plants) contain toxins that vary among plant species. The toxic levels are generally low enough so that they don't kill the animal, but nibbling herbivores will avoid that plant in the future if the taste is obnoxious and digestion is difficult. Animals typically diversify their diets to get all the nutrients they need, and so this limits the intake of any one toxin, which is to the advantage of both plants and animals.

Toxin production is biologically expensive and somewhat dangerous, so plant tissues generally contain either a high level of toxins or else they grow rapidly. Rapidly growing and easily replaced tissue, such as leaves, would thus be less toxic than the more indispensable plant parts, such as stems and roots. If the plant has to give up something to herbivores in the ecological battle, it tends to give them easily replaced leaves. Although we humans eat a variety of leaves, we also eat the more toxic roots and stems (rather than the leaves) of some vegetables, such as carrots, onions, asparagus, broccoli, and cauliflower.

Organisms differ in their susceptibility to toxins. Immature rapidly growing organisms are generally less able to tolerate toxins than mature organisms. Many children thus consider the strong toxin-related odors and flavors of onions, broccoli, and similar vegetables to be obnoxious while adults consider them spicy and piquant.

While children can often successfully (and perhaps honestly) complain to their parents about the bad taste of certain vegetables, an embryo has a more serious problem. Embryos absorb whatever the mother eats, and a rapidly growing embryo is especially vulnerable to toxins. The embryonic solution apparently is to send a complaining chemical message to the mother that results in what is commonly called morning sickness. The result is that pregnant women are often nauseated by spicy foods, and they avoid them to the benefit of the embryo. The good news is that Nulman (Morning sickness, 2009) discovered that children age three to seven whose mothers had suffered intensely from morning sickness tended to score higher on intelligence tests than those who did not. Profet (1992) reported that women who don't suffer from pregnancy nausea are more likely to miscarry or bear children with birth defects. Similarly, pregnant women who use high levels of alcohol or other toxic drugs risk disorders in their children, such as fetal alcohol syndrome.

I suspect that most parents don't realize that some vegetables have low levels of toxicity that their children can detect, but they often intuitively make such vegetables more palatable by masking the sharp flavors, such as by placing sugar on carrots and cheese sauce on broccoli and cauliflower.

This raises an interesting issue. Do children who most dislike such vegetables have a lower tolerance for the toxins than children who like the vegetables? Can forcing children to eat something that nauseates them result in strong negative adult rejection? Should children be taught to put up with a little discomfort if the disliked food provides important nutrient values? Good questions. No simple answers.

Food preferences are obviously more complicated than toxin levels. For example, smell is more important than taste in the recognition and selection of many foods, and the common use of herbs and spices enhances this process. Cultural differences in odor preferences also exist. Many Asians consider the smell of cheese to be obnoxious, and the odors of sauerkraut and pickles similarly attract and repulse different people. On the other hand, everyone seems to like the odor of vanilla (which is somewhat similar to breast milk).

Our brain can recognize about 10,000 different odors that are created from perhaps 30 different kinds of molecules. Most odors are combinations of molecules that enter our nose in the air we breathe and then attach to receptors. Smell is the only sensory system that isn't initially processed in our brain's **thalamus**. In smell, the current combination of molecular inputs is sent directly to the **olfactory bulb** in the front of our brain, and it's then relayed to various emotion and interpretive systems.

Language functions similarly in that our brain can create words by differentially combining the few dozen phonemes that our auditory system can recognize, and so it can create languages of hundreds of thousands of words. Smell is thus a kind of molecular language that quickly analyzes and immediately determines the value of potential food before it enters our mouth. Note that our nose is placed directly above our mouth.

Overcoming Aversions. I completely lost my appetite three weeks into chemotherapy and radiation treatments for esophageal cancer, and for the first time in my life, I had a sense of what it must be like to be anorexic. I previously had no food aversions, and I was intrigued by new food combinations or preparations, but suddenly my appetite was gone. I was actually repulsed by even the thought of food. I realized as a mature adult that this was a temporary phenomenon, and that I needed to eat, so I forced myself to eat the few foods that weren't totally repulsive. But, I finally had empathy for young people who look forward in horror to a lifetime without appetite.

Getting children involved in food production and preparation can help reduce their aversion to certain vegetables. Teachers who develop classroom gardens that include vegetables commonly disliked by students discover that students will typically sample things that they grew. Involving children in the selection and preparation of home meals similarly encourages the exploration of new tastes. Such developmental prompts enhance children's maturation into adults who are oriented to the positive natural and cultural elements of food and nutrition.

I had the common childhood aversion to parsley, carefully removing each miniscule piece from the mashed potatoes or rice my mother had made. One day, she simply asked me to get some sprigs of parsley out of the garden by kneeling down to smell them before picking them and to select only the ones with the most pleasant smell. When I brought them to the kitchen, she showed me how to use a knife to mince them, and she told me that she wouldn't put any parsley in the potatoes I ate if I didn't want any. For the first time in my life, I nibbled on a sprig of parsley, and then I said she didn't have to do that. I would eat the parsleyed potatoes.

Many decades later, we have a large pot of parsley growing on our deck, and I understand how artfully my mother had eliminated my aversion to parsley.

8

The Unexpected

From Joys and Toys to Fears and Tears

Our brain's emotion and attention systems are especially tuned to the novel and unexpected, which is much of what a child's brain confronts. Although children seem to prefer consistency in their lives, they soon realize that unexpected events occur. Some, such as gifts on special occasions, bring happiness. Others, such as the death of a pet, bring sadness. Childhood nurturing should thus help children respond appropriately to unexpected abnormal events, from the excitement of going on a family vacation to winning a school award and from a disagreement with a friend to the death of a grandparent.

Chapter 4 reported that our basic internal survival systems are functional at birth. For example, children can breathe and drink and then unconsciously move the ingested air and fluids through their bodies, but adults have to carry them until they can walk. Children similarly can't immediately recognize and respond to many unexpected dangers and opportunities, so nurturing adults must identify, model, and explain appropriate responses to such challenges.

The mirror neuron system, which automatically simulates and then replicates the observed movements of others, enhances the childhood mastery of the basic movements we use to avoid dangers and embrace opportunities. The child observes the adult response and learns from the experience.

Children need to feel confident that adults will provide the resources and security they need and patiently teach them how to function independently. Parents and other relatives enhance the beginning of a child's maturation by focusing principally on family values and routines. Teachers expand the cultural range when the child enters school.

The elementary school's two principal tasks seem to be (1) to teach children the basic regularities and irregularities that define our various communication codes and cultural systems and (2) to enhance social maturation, especially how to get along with classmates who have different values and/or behavioral patterns. Family and school thus collaborate in providing children with a sense of how their immediate and extended worlds function.

EMOTION AND FEELINGS

No is one of the first words that most children learn and use. It's an important concept, as it communicates that something is disagreeable and/or dangerous. A child's *no* typically alerts the parent or teacher to something the child considers disagreeable, such as being asked to eat broccoli or complete a school assignment. An adult *no* typically signals potential danger to the child, such as to not play with a knife or to not rush into the street to retrieve a ball.

Chapter 2 introduced the related concepts of emotion and feelings, which constitute our brain's arousal system. Let's continue our exploration of the central role this system plays in the life of a child.

Think of our emotional system as a biological thermostat that unconsciously alerts the rest of our brain to variations from normality from within and outside of our body. It's composed of a collection of structures commonly called the **limbic system** (located in the area surrounding the brainstem). If a stimulus doesn't immediately trigger a reflexive response, the emotional arousal will activate our feelings, which consciously determine the level of significance. If the challenge seems important, our attention system will identify its dynamics and then activate relevant problem-solving systems that consciously respond to the challenge. Almost everything we do thus begins with emotional arousal.

Emotion often publicly manifests itself in facial, body, and speech displays. For example, we can detect upwards of 300 different emotional expressions that the forty-four human facial muscles regulate. It's often important to inform others of the kind and severity of the challenge that confronts us, and it is similarly important to recognize such emotional displays in others. Think of the reflexive cry and upraised arms of a startled helpless infant that signal the need for parental help.

As indicated above, an emotional arousal can lead to conscious feelings that elevate our involvement with the challenge and bias the subsequent conscious design of our response. Although we typically display our emotional state, we'll hide our feelings from others whenever it's advantageous to not signal what we plan to do.

Emotion researchers have identified a couple dozen discrete emotional states that exist along intensity continua, such as from apprehension to fear to terror or from annoyance to anger to rage. Some emotions are blends of simultaneously activated emotions. Trust and fear combine to create submission, and trust and joy blend into love. Although many researchers consider fear, anger, disgust, surprise, sadness, and joy to be the primary emotions, other classification systems have also been proposed. Some emotional states imply social relationships, such as sympathy, guilt, jealousy, envy, and gratitude. Our processing system for emotions and feelings is thus complex.

For example, I can think of being in a state of current contentment (mental equilibrium or bodily homeostasis).

My sensory system detects an emotionally charged stimulus from inside or outside my body.

What occurs is an immediate analysis of the challenge and the current state of my body/brain. My basic concerns: What are my current levels of alertness, strength, and energy? Are they such that I'm capable of successfully confronting this unexpected potentially dangerous or opportunistic challenge and, further, am I motivated to do it? If the analysis is optimistic, a positive state will emerge (such as joy, anticipation, or trust). On the other hand, if the analysis is pessimistic, a negative state will emerge (such as fear, anger, or grief). I'll thus move confidently forward in the design and execution of a response, or I'll warily avert the problem. Optimistic states seem to be principally processed in the left frontal lobes, and pessimistic states are mostly processed in the right frontal lobes.

If the analysis doesn't clearly place me in either category, an uncertain state emerges (and surprise, confusion, and anticipation are examples of this state). The traditional fight/flight/freeze categories used to describe behavior in stressful situations thus also describe emotional arousal and the emergence of feelings. We adults can often metacognitively sense this back-and-forth discussion going on in our brain while we're trying to decide on such things as a risky opportunity or what to do about a suddenly malfunctioning appliance.

Our innate temperament can also bias the analysis and the resulting emotional state. Temperament emerges by the age of two and is generally categorized as either bold/uninhibited, anxious/inhibited, or somewhere in between. The bold tend to go toward challenges in optimistic curiosity, and the anxious tend to move away in pessimistic wariness.

Mood (which tends to exist over a shorter period from a few hours to a few days) can similarly affect this analysis in the direction of the positive or negative mood we're experiencing. We may thus eagerly tackle a problem on Tuesday that we would avoid on Thursday.

Drugs, illness, and beliefs (religious, political, etc.) can also bias the accuracy of this analysis and the consequent conscious optimistic or pessimistic feelings that result. We may thus incorrectly believe that we're capable or incapable of meeting certain challenges.

These positive and negative emotional states often return after the fact, when we assess the results of our decision. Emotions such as elation and pride follow success, and disappointment and guilt follow defeat. The emotionally tagged memories of the experience pop up when subsequent similar challenges occur, and they can then bias that analysis.

Children tend to seek adult help if they consider a challenge to be beyond their capabilities, and so it's important for nurturing adults to use careful observation and helpful questions to guide them through the process. It's also important to help children make retrospective analyses of their feelings and responses so they can better develop their ability to understand and regulate their affective systems.

Emotional arousal is thus a complex, basically innate system that needs constant adult nurturing during childhood in order for the unconscious and conscious elements to blend and mature into self-regulation—for example, to choose the possibility of a better but delayed reward over an immediate reward. Effective adult modeling and a continuing adult-child dialogue define emotional nurturing at its best. A principal additional task, of course, is to help children identify and focus on the cause of the emotional arousal. That's attention.

ATTENTION

Attention is a complex cognitive system that selects and temporarily focuses on key emotionally important elements in an often-confusing environment and then maintains goal-directed behavior in highly distracting situations. It thus psychologically separates a current emotionally significant foreground from the less significant background. Think of the frame on a picture, the zoom lens on a camera, traffic arrows, and the stage in an auditorium as technologies that help to direct our attention by separating foreground from background.

Our attentional system is composed of three distinct but interconnected neural networks, each of which actively carries out specific attentional functions (Posner & Rothbart, 2007).

The *alerting network* maintains the conscious level of alertness and vigilance that allows us to focus on potentially important sensory information. The network begins in a midbrain area called the **locus coeruleus** and spreads into the parietal and frontal lobes.

Vigilance maintains a sustained focus on something currently deemed important while ignoring small, random, potentially distracting sensory stimuli. Conversely, a major distraction may shift our focus of attention. We typically can simultaneously attend to several noncompeting events (such as to look at a person while conversing and putting on a coat), but not to competing events (such as to simultaneously carry on live and phone conversations).

As remarkable as our vigilance system is, it isn't very effective at sustaining attention on tasks that are oriented to precise details and contain only subtle environmental shifts. Many educational activities unfortunately require students to maintain vigilant attention in such situations (such as while solving a page of many similar math problems). Vigilance is an important component in most games children play (from tag to video games), so they seem to have an almost innate sense that they need to develop the system. Many accidents involve lapses in vigilance.

The *orienting network* disengages us from what we were attending to and focuses us on a new challenge. The network is centered in several areas of the parietal lobes and in the visual area of the frontal lobes. As indicated above, we generally shift our attention to objects and events that contrast sharply with our current focus, and we ignore (or merely monitor) steady states, subtle differences, and gradual changes that don't carry a sense of immediacy. For example, we tend to ignore a constant temperature, but we attend to a sudden change.

Our environment, however, is replete with serious subtle and gradual dangers (such as pollution). They're emotionally significant, but we tend to focus on them only when a high contrast catastrophe (such as a toxic spill) occurs. The *news* is about the unusual, not the normal, so it reports a single freeway pile-up of 10 cars, but not the perhaps 100 individual fender-benders that occurred in the same general area that day. Graphs and time-lapse photography are technological aids we've developed to observe changes that occur too gradually to activate our biological emotion and attention systems.

The *executive attention network* is located principally in the frontal lobes and cingulate. Because the frontal lobes of children haven't yet matured, nurturing adults often must guide or even assume a child's executive attention functions. This is especially evident in elementary classrooms. Teachers typically tell their students what to attend to and for how long, and they often give advice on how best to accomplish the assignment.

The executive attention network draws heavily on memory to recognize the identity of a new challenge (foreground), determine its significance, and separate it from the background information. This is typically an efficient process that draws on established responses, but we do confront situations in which it's not obvious what we should focus on within a confusing setting. In such situations, our executive attention system must consciously make the decision, such as to respond to a novel situation that will require planning and decision making, to alter a habitual response, or to correct an error.

It's also often not clear whether a challenge is a danger or opportunity, or which of several current challenges is most important, so this network is critical to the resolution of such ambiguities. A dysfunctional executive attention network may attempt to solve the wrong problem or to solve problems we don't understand. This error occurs at all levels, from within individual brains to the sets of interacting brains that constitute a company or government.

Our working brain (or working memory) is an important part of this system. It's a fragile limited-capacity buffer that allows us to briefly attend to and hold a few units of information during their use or while determining their importance. It's about things that are immediately important but not so important that we need to remember them for the rest of our life, such as a phone number while dialing or a stranger's name during a brief conversation. The limited capacity of our working brain is useful, as it forces us to combine related bits of information into larger units by identifying similarities, differences, and patterns that can simplify and consolidate an otherwise large and confusing sensory field. Vocabulary categories emerged out of this cognitive ability.

Our three-part attention system thus moves us from arousal to focus in preparation for decision and action. It's a sort of zoom lens that can zoom in to identify and carefully examine details (foreground) or zoom out to scan the context (background).

Children differ in their attentional preferences and in their ability to regulate attention. What an odd world it would be if we were all culturally and cognitively cloned, with the same interests and abilities. The individual differences that nurturing adults thus confront are challenging, but to complain about them is like a custodian complaining that the floors are dirty. Human variability defines our nurturing assignment.

ATTENTIONAL DISORDERS

Attention deficit disorder (ADD) is a class of behavioral disorders characterized by persistent inattention, impulsiveness, and often hyperactivity. ADD is generally considered a childhood disorder that affects up to 10% of the population—and three times as many boys as girls—but it can persist into adult life.

Although educators have been especially concerned about ADHD (attention deficit hyperactivity disorder) because of its negative impact on classroom life, it's important to realize that malfunctions in one or more of the subsystems that regulate attention can lead to many different mental illnesses and learning handicaps (such as anxiety, autism, bipolar disorder, dyslexia, hyperactivity, mental retardation, obsessive-compulsive disorder, and schizophrenia). Medications and behavioral interventions exist to help those whose deficits in one or more elements of the attentional system are related to chemical imbalances, developmentally weak neuronal pathways, and/or learned inappropriate behavior patterns.

Recent optimistic research (Posner & Rothbart, 2007) suggests that we're entering a period in which potential attention disorders can be diagnosed early in life, so successful interventions can more probably occur during the child's developmental years. The Electronic Resources section contains related useful websites on attention disorders for parents and educators.

Sudden Spontaneous Influences

Rousell (2007) suggests that sudden, unpredictable, emotionally powerful experiences can dramatically change our perspective of the world and/or ourselves, and they can bias the development of our personality. Our awareness of these events typically remains elusive because such Spontaneous Influence Events (SIEs) occur instantly and unexpectedly, and they trigger the automatic short-term activation of a state of extreme suggestibility. For example, a person struggling for a solution to a vexing problem may suddenly discover it within the offhand remark of a friend. Conversely, a person who is proud of an accomplishment may interpret the seemingly lukewarm response of a friend as depreciating and so lose confidence in her ability.

These positive or negative events are imprinted into neural networks that bias our mind to interpret related new experiences within the context of the SIE. A self-perpetuating cycle thus ensues that takes place outside conscious awareness. We may remember the initial triggering event but not understand its influence until much later—if ever. A single childhood experience of attempted molestation by a stranger might thus trigger an extended aversion to anyone who resembles the molester. Similarly, a single positive comment from an adult at a key moment could improve a child's self-image.

Rousell (2007) suggests that we are often emotionally primed for these life-changing events, which, as indicated above, may be nothing more than a simple offhand remark or activity that certainly wasn't intended to profoundly affect our life. A comment made on one occasion without effect could thus become an SIE in another. The critical factor for an SIE to occur is the recipient's receptivity and intense emotional arousal. We frequently replay an SIE interaction in our mind as we connect it to subsequent events. That's not surprising, because SIEs can lead to vocational, bonding, and other important choices. Former students have recalled specific comments or incidents in my courses that profoundly affected them, and I had no recollection of the events. I suspect that the same thing has occurred to many of you.

It's thus important to understand the SIE concept and its effect because the phenomenon helps us to understand the events that shape our lives and the impact we often unwittingly have on the lives of others. Not surprisingly, the susceptibility that can activate a SIE is also operative within hypnosis.

Children are especially susceptible to SIEs because their model of themselves and the world is still evolving. A child's perception of an event is very malleable when caught during or shortly after such an event. During that critical window, positive adult nurturing may produce subsequent constructive self-perpetuating streams of events. Because children often look to people they consider more mature for guidance, it's important that parents, teachers, counselors, and others who work with the vulnerable continually recognize the potential for susceptibility and respond appropriately.

Simply asking children to provide their perspective of the event if their body language suggests a SIE is a beginning.

This suggests that a principal nurturing task is to provide children with a strong sense of normality and regularity in home and school. Teaching and modeling appropriate behavior does that, and this includes everything from regular meals at home to learning the multiplication tables at school. Parents tend to help solve a child's personal problems, and teachers tend to help solve social problems. It's scary for a child to be unable to respond competently to unexpected events, and almost everything is unexpected in the lives of the very young.

I mentioned in Chapter 7 that I had recently been diagnosed and treated for esophageal cancer. The diagnosis came as a complete surprise to me since I didn't have any of the common risk factors. I was mature enough to respond appropriately to such an unexpected development, but children typically aren't. I asked questions, and I investigated cancer so that what was mysterious became something I now understand. When illness occurs during childhood, however, a nurturing adult must provide the child with such useful supportive information.

Childhood Illness

From Short to Long Term

We're biologically excellent but not perfect. The evolutionary solution to the issue of human longevity is a cost/benefit ratio that historically allowed most of us to reach reproductive maturity, and then to maintain reasonable health and productivity until our children matured. Because a longer lifespan would require our body/brain systems to be much more robust and biologically expensive than they are, our solution was to reach beyond our biological limitations. We did this through recent technological advances in medicine and diet that extended the average U.S. lifespan by 30 years during the 20th century. We thus now live longer, but we do so at an immense technological cost that creates continuing contentious societal issues.

The big three medical problems have historically involved *invasions* (infectious disease, pollutants, drugs, and wounds), *insurrections* (developmental disorders, malignancies, and organ breakdowns), and the inevitability of *death*. The medical profession has done quite well with invasions, seems to be progressing effectively with insurrections, and has increased the U.S. lifespan to an average of 78 years.

Our parents' genetic history and the state of their health affect us from conception on. We share our mother's experiences during her pregnancy—the food she eats, illnesses and accidents she has, and hormonal variations she experiences. Elements of this shared life continue after birth: Breast-fed infants continue to share their mother's diet. The parents' emotional states and behaviors affect their children. A family shares the same living conditions.

Although colds and flu remain common, serious illness and death during childhood have become atypical in our culture. The annual death rate for children under 14 is only about one in 5,000 in the United States. Still, illness, disability, and accidents can temporarily or permanently rob children of important elements of childhood, and they tend to respond differently than adults to health problems. It's thus important that children develop a functional understanding of the cause and nature of health problems and that adults know how to nurture children who are beset by them. Let's explore key basic elements of health and illness that children must understand if they are to mature into responsible citizens who will have to solve the complex health problems that confront our society. What follows is a functional introduction to the malfunctions that our excellent but not perfect body and brain periodically experience. Pass it on to the children you nurture.

The Electronic Resources section in the back of the book provides links to excellent nontechnical websites that focus on individual types of illnesses and disabilities, which provide specific useful information and practical advice for parents and educators that go well beyond this chapter's more general focus.

INVASIONS

Chapter 7 suggested that we're basically a 27-foot tube with a body wrapped around it. The flexible mantle of skin that covers our body is only one-tenth of an inch thick, but it plays primary protective roles in warding off infection and in maintaining our body's shape and internal temperature. At about eight pounds and 22 square feet (for an adult), it's the largest organ of our bodies, and one of the most important in understanding the nature of invasive illness.

The dermis, the deeper of our skin's two layers, has a base of fat that cushions our body from external pressure and insulates it from cold temperatures. The dermis also contains such protective elements as hair follicles, sweat glands, a circulatory system for nourishment and waste removal, and sensory cells that recognize variations in touch and temperature.

The epidermis is our skin's outer layer. Blood vessels in the dermis nourish the lower epidermal area where new skin cells constantly develop. These emerging cells push out the older cells, which then change their composition and shape because they've lost their blood supply and cellular fluids. These now flattened dead cells form the waterproof outer part of our skin, and so serve as an effective barrier to infection and injury. Our skin's surface gets sloughed off by constant environmental buffeting, and what was underneath becomes surface. The process from new cell to sloughed-off skin takes about a month, a continual skin rejuvenation that is essential in the healing of wounds. Children might think of a scab as temporary skin over a wound, something that will similarly slough off when the permanent regeneration occurring underneath is completed.

To place our protective needs and regulatory systems in context, it's important to understand that we have two related internal systems that recognize and respond to the dangers and opportunities our environment poses.

1. Our skull-centered brain is composed of over a trillion highly interconnected neurons and **glial support cells**. It integrates and responds to environmental challenges that our sensory system can process, such as the search for food.

2. Our diffused immune system is composed of an equally immense number of (mostly free-floating) cells

that emerge out of our **lymphatic system** but are spread throughout our body. It responds to the several pounds of invisible **microbes** and pollutants that enter and inhabit our body, identifying and destroying those that are dangerous. The *dangerous* microbes (commonly called germs, although the scientific term is *pathogens*) enter our body in search of an environment that will enhance their survival, albeit perhaps to the detriment of our health and survival. It's also important for children to understand that many microbes (such as those that aid digestion) are very helpful and even necessary to our survival.

So our very interconnected brain responds to the larger, visible external challenges we confront, and our very diffused immune system and other protective systems (such as stomach acid and lung mucus) respond to the tiny, invisible internal challenges that enter our body through wounds and digestive and respiratory openings. We've also technologically augmented our *immune* capabilities through vaccinations prior to a potential infection and through antibiotics after infection. Advances in food preservation and preparation, water treatment, and personal hygiene have similarly reduced the current risk of infections.

A successful response to many of life's challenges requires the collaboration of our brain and immune system. For example, in multiple sclerosis, our immune system doesn't properly differentiate between body tissue and foreign substances, and so it destroys the myelin insulation on motor neurons. This impairs mobility and thus causes conscious life changes. Similarly, poor cognitive decisions often lead to accidents, and our immune system then wards off potential infections in the resulting wounds.

Chapter 7 reported that we have a special protective system called the blood-brain barrier that limits materials that can enter our brain. It thus blocks out most potential bacterial infections, but it also complicates the challenge of getting therapeutic drugs into our brain in order to alleviate brain disorders. Encephalitis is an example of a brain infection—a serious inflammation of brain tissue caused either by a primary infection or by the extension of an infectious disease (such as mumps or measles).

Invasive health problems don't come only from tiny organisms and pollutants. Hitting others in anger; playing with sharp, hot, or cold objects; and taking risks that can lead to accidents are common invasive behaviors that can negatively affect a child's skin and body. Sexual molestation is another form of psychological and physical invasion that typically involves inappropriate seduction, touching, and insertion behaviors.

We can similarly think of hurtful language as psychologically invasive. Profanities, obscenities, racial and ethnic slurs, and other forms of defamation can negatively affect the self-concept of a developing child. The stress that results from chronic verbal abuse can be as unhealthy as physically invasive disease. For example, our immune system becomes less effective during periods of extended stress, and this can lead to infections that our body would otherwise fight off.

Drug use generally begins during adolescence, but children should incorporate the concepts of drugs into their understanding of the negative effects of invasive substances on body systems. Suggesting that illicit drugs are an analog of germs might be a good way to begin.

INSURRECTIONS

Sometimes we're our own enemy, and illness and injury come from within. These problems can occur because of a genetic disorder, a developmental delay, a malignancy, a breakdown in an aging organ or system, or a foolish decision. For example, drugs are an invasive problem, but the initial conscious decision that leads to the addiction occurs within the addict's brain.

We begin our existence when parental sperm and egg cells join. For what it's worth, the male sperm cell is the smallest cell in our body, and the female egg is the largest. The combined cell divides into two cells, and they divide again into four cells. Thus begins life's incredible expansion by division. Estimates of the final number of cells in the human body are in the tens of trillions. It's certainly an immense number of cells, but our body is also host to perhaps 10 times that many microbes at any given time.

These body cells organize themselves into 10 major **organ systems**, each of which contains several different but related organs. So, our body is kind of like a house with several dozen inhabitants (plus a zillion freeloading microbes) all trying to get along. Even elementary school-aged children know that a single dysfunctional person in a group can make life miserable for the others, and a dysfunctional organ system can similarly do that to the rest of a body/brain.

Developmental disorders that emerge during pregnancy or early childhood typically result from malfunctions in a single system or a related set of systems. The cause is typically a genetic malfunction or is the result of something that occurred in the womb or shortly after birth. Some of these disorders are still poorly understood, and effective treatments have yet to emerge, but a functional understanding of what is known about a disorder is a child's first step in knowing how best to deal with it.

Mobility is a central human property, so it's a factor in many childhood developmental or acquired disabilities. Cerebral palsy, muscular dystrophy, and spina bifida come immediately to mind, but being blind or deaf also creates mobility problems, as do asthma and congenital heart defects.

Movement involves more than the actual regulation of body mobility, however. Chapter 2 reported that our brain's principal task is to plan, regulate, and predict movements, so some (principally frontal lobe) brain disorders result in poor planning and predicting. Our frontal lobes don't mature until late adolescence, so one could think of all children as developmentally delayed with respect to the movement spectrum. Most move easily by the time they enter school, but they often plan and predict poorly. Adults thus serve as a movement-regulating influence until a child's frontal lobes mature.

Chapter 8 reported that attention is central to all movement behavior and that many illnesses are related to attention disorders. For example, anxiety disorders are a major health problem for children. Anxiety often manifests in an inability to plan an activity and/or in unfounded fears about the outcome of the activity. Similarly, autistic children are unable to infer the intentions of others, so they can't predict the outcome of social behavior.

Cancer may well be the childhood *insurrection* illness that most concerns us. Well over a half-million people die annually from it in the United States. Humans suffer from many different kinds of cancers, but all result from uncontrolled cell division in the cancerous area. It manifests itself as a solid mass of cells (a tumor) in a specific body area, or as changes in the composition of blood (such as white blood cell increases in leukemia). Cancers can spread (metastasize) to other nearby or distant areas via the circulatory of lymphatic system. It's one thing to get a cancer diagnosis after living a long, happy, and productive life—as I did—and it's quite another thing to get the diagnosis as a child.

Cancer is the major cause of childhood death from disease, with well over 2,000 dying annually from it in the United States. Twenty-five percent of the elementary schools in the United States have a student suffering from cancer. The most common form of childhood cancer is leukemia, a cancer of the blood that begins in bone marrow, where blood cells are made. Childhood leukemia was formerly fatal for most children, but 80% now survive. Many adult cancers are related to lifestyle choices, but childhood cancer has a randomness about it that spares no demographic group or geographic region. One problem with the treatment of childhood cancer is that 80% of the diagnoses occur when it's already in an advanced stage, as compared with 20% in adults.

DEATH

Death is inevitable, but it occurred sooner for most people during my childhood than it does now. All four of my grandparents had died by the time I was born in 1927, and schoolmates died from such infectious diseases as smallpox and measles during my elementary school years. Vaccinations have now virtually eradicated most of these diseases.

A request from the March of Dimes in today's mail reminds me that its original purpose about 70 years ago was to seek funds to treat and cure polio (poliomyelitis), a dreaded disease that had crippled President Franklin D. Roosevelt, and annually paralyzed and killed many children. With polio now virtually eradicated in the United States, the March of Dimes has shifted its focus to birth defects and other infant health problems (and they now prefer dollars to dimes).

Child deaths in developed countries are now more apt to occur because of accidents—the major cause of death in U.S. children. Many of these involve motor vehicle accidents that also cause life-changing injuries to other surviving passengers.

As most children are part of a larger extended family, I suspect that mortality becomes a reality for many of them when grandparents, uncles, and aunts die. However, because such relatives are apt to live at a distance, the child's relationship with the deceased may well have been limited to periodic family gatherings. Further, death within one's extended family is often gradual as the deteriorating condition worsens. Children may thus only know a once vibrant person during the final frailty of cognitive and/or motor decline, and so they may have trouble understanding the grief their parents feel.

Death on television and in computer games tends to be immediate and violent, and unusual and noteworthy deaths are replayed frequently in the media. Death in the mass media typically provides little if any context. People appear briefly on screen and die. Except for children who live on farms and/or hunt and fish, death in our diet similarly lacks context. The meat we eat conveys no relationship to the live animal it once was.

It may well be that for many children the death of a pet provides the context for life and death that they rarely experience otherwise.

THE NURTURING TASKS OF PARENTS AND EDUCATORS

Parents and educators have separate but also collaborative responsibilities in helping children (1) to develop a functional understanding of illness and death and (2) to respond effectively to a child's current disabling condition.

Parents should provide the recommended vaccinations and responsible care during short-term and chronic illness, and they should help their child develop hygiene and behavioral habits that reduce the danger of illness.

Educators should create a school environment that reduces the potential for accidents, conflict, and the spread of infection, and encourages acceptance of all students for who they are.

The concept of unconditional love, discussed in Chapter 5, is thus fundamental to both groups when dealing with children who are ill—to love them for who they are and not for how they behave. Adults should communicate a simple genuine acceptance that focuses on children's abilities rather than on their disabilities.

Although illnesses differ considerably, avoid thinking comparatively: that one debilitating condition is better or worse than another. The illness a child has is the illness the child has, and that's the illness the two of you are confronting.

A central tenet of this chapter is that children have a right to a functional understanding of what their illness is and what's being done to alleviate it. Adults should thus provide honest, direct, and nontechnical information. If an elementary teacher explains the basics of a student's illness, the class will be better able to respond appropriately to the ill student, and they will also be better informed if any of them subsequently has the same or a similar health problem.

It's not only a matter of providing children with useful information, but also a matter of listening carefully to their questions and feelings, which may be considerably different from what we expect. Realize also that they may interpret terms differently than adults. For example, if we refer to anesthesia as putting the patient *to sleep,* a child may relate that to a veterinarian putting a very sick pet *to sleep.*

Parents and educators should thus collaborate in providing children with a functional understanding of illness and death. This chapter provides a general introduction to the concept, and, as indicated earlier, the Electronic Resources section in the back of the book provides links to excellent websites that provide useful, specific information and practical nurturing advice on the wide range of illnesses and related problems (such as sexual molestation) that parents and educators confront. The website of the National Center on Birth Defects and Developmental Disabilities is an excellent example of a comprehensive source of specific information and advice on such disorders.

Parents and educators should also collaborate to ensure that children get at least an hour a day of the kind of physical activity that enhances the health of their body. This activity should incorporate aerobic, muscle-building, and bone-strengthening activities. Hiking and running, swimming and skateboarding, jumping rope and climbing ropes are a few of many activities that enhance physical fitness. Informal neighborhood soccer, softball, and other games with friends add powerful affective and social values in addition to the benefits of physical exercise.

Inclusion. Until relatively recently, students with serious disabilities were hidden from view in special education settings, or else they were institutionalized. Technological advances (such as self-propelled wheelchairs), handicapped access laws, and the emergence of the concept of inclusive classrooms are examples of societal changes that now allow many students who are ill or disabled to attend mainstream inclusive classrooms.

Inclusive education thinks beyond the needs of special education students. It respects the current condition and capabilities of all students. It insists that students benefit from the constant presence of others whose life challenges differ from theirs. Stereotyping and prejudice tend to decrease when we interact on a personal level with people who differ from us, and this is also true beyond the classroom.

Recall the initial fussing over the cost of curb cuts and entrance ramps when they were mandated to help the relatively small number of people who then used self-propelled wheelchairs. But the fussing stopped when folks realized that these access changes also help parents with baby carriages, people with wheeled luggage, bicyclists, the blind, the elderly, and many others who view steps as a barrier. When a society helps the few who truly need help, everyone else also eventually benefits.

What's normal to one person isn't necessarily what's normal to another.

Intelligence, Creativity, and the Arts

From What Is to What Could Be

One of the major curiosities about humans is the great amount of time and energy we spend in creating, relaying, and attending to stories that both the sender and receiver know aren't true. It makes survival sense to share true information, but fictional narrative seems intellectually and culturally pointless. And yet, fiction has been a dominant force in all cultures—from short jokes and parables to extended novels and various dramatic forms. We often add illustrations, gestures, music, and dance to enhance a story's emotional impact and narrative flow. We even try to bolster arguments with fabricated anecdotes. Does a day ever go by in which fictional narrative is absent from our life?

More curiously, even though children have much factual information to master, their enculturation is replete with made-up stories—from fables to fairy tales, from Santa Claus to the Easter Bunny. Children can learn much from true narratives, but what can they possibly learn from fiction?

The answer that's emerging is that fictional narrative plays a central role in the juvenile development and adult maintenance of our cognitive processes. Brian Boyd's (2009) thought-provoking *On the Origin of Stories: Evolution, Cognition, and Fiction* is an excellent example of imaginative explorations that now seek to unravel such longstanding enigmas of human thought and behavior.

Boyd considers fiction to be an important art form, and the arts to be a major venue for developing and maintaining human cognition, cooperation, and creativity. Fictional narrative incorporates all three of these elements: we have a brain that can process ambiguity, we're a social species, and we continually confront novel challenges.

This chapter will explore the developmental role of (1) intelligence, the level of cognitive competence a person demonstrates; (2) creativity, the ability to respond effectively to novel challenges; and (3) the arts, the playing field on which intelligence and creativity develop—a playing field replete with fictional narrative.

INTELLIGENCE

We've long been interested in the nature and development of intelligence, and this interest escalated during the past 25 years. The multiple intelligences theories of Howard Gardner (1983), Robert Sternberg (1985), and David Perkins (1995) were especially influential in shaping contemporary educational thought and practice. Intelligence had previously been viewed as a unitary cognitive property that could be quantified and placed somewhere along a general intelligence scale that uses 100 as an average score for a given age (IQ, intelligence quotient).

Multiple intelligence theorists argue that intelligence encompasses several separate but interactive types of cognitive abilities, and the nature of the current challenge determines the combination that will be activated to resolve it. It kind of reminds me of the plumber who arrived yesterday with a truck full of tools and repair materials. After inspecting the problem, he got and used only what he needed from his truck.

Another possibility of course is that each of us has a general level of intelligence (such as an IQ score) and that our various more specific cognitive abilities (such as multiple intelligences categories) correlate at differing levels with our general intelligence.

The theorist's perspective of the organization of the world and cognition determines the nature and format of the proposed intelligence categories. For example, Gardner's categories have a *noun* perspective (personal/social identity, space/place, and time/sequence) and Sternberg's categories have a *verb* perspective (be analytical, creative, and practical in the solution of problems). Appendix B provides a more extensive nontechnical explanation of prominent theories of multiple intelligences.

The several theories of multiple intelligences argue that the robustness of a person's various *intelligences* may vary, and that this could affect the effectiveness of the response to a specific challenge. For example, a person might be above average in linguistic ability but below average in mathematical ability, or be very practical but not very creative.

Intelligence as an absolute concept is thus difficult to define, but all theorists propose definitions and explanations. Jeff Hawkins' (Hawkins & Blakeslee, 2004) proposal is especially intriguing for those interested in the emergence of intelligence during childhood and in the role that fiction plays in understanding reality.

Hawkins believes that the hierarchical organization and conscious operation of our brain's cerebral cortex provide the key to understanding and enhancing intelligence. Chapter 3 described the horizontal, vertical, and systems organization of the cortex, but a brief summary here may be helpful in understanding his theory.

The Human Brain, Summarized. Each of the six horizontal layers of the cortex processes important general functions, such as layer four's role in receiving incoming information.

The billions of cortical neurons are also organized vertically into several hundred million hair-thin columns of about 100 connected neurons that extend through the six cortical layers and interconnect with other cortical columns and brain areas. Each column (and aggregate of related columns) has a distinct function, such as to respond to a specific tone or line segment or to move a specific muscle, but the columns are highly interconnected via the underlying axonal white matter.

The cortex itself is divided into two hemispheres, each of which encompasses four lobes. The three sensory lobes in the back half of the hemisphere receive raw sensory information and combine it into a perceptual interpretation of the external environment. The frontal lobe determines and executes a response if one is needed.

The two hemispheres collaborate on the analysis and resolution of most challenges, but each has specialized functions. The four right hemisphere lobes take the lead in processing novel challenges and developing creative solutions. The four left hemisphere lobes do the same in processing familiar challenges and activating established successful responses.

Sensory Input. Our sensory and motor systems connect us to the outside environment. Although our various senses seem distinct, Hawkins (Hawkins & Blakeslee, 2004) argues that our brain processes them all as related spatial/temporal patterns. Recall that movement is our brain's defining property, and movement results from the expenditure of energy in space over time.

Spatial patterns occur when multiple receptors in a sensory system are simultaneously stimulated (such as by the notes of a chord or the elements of a scene). Temporal patterns occur when such patterns change over time (such as in tone and chord sequences from a melody or movement occurring within a scene).

Initially meaningless sensory information becomes perceptually integrated and meaningful as it moves hierarchically through our highly interconnected cortex—shapes, textures, and colors combine to form a face; sounds become melodic sequences that become a song—and the observed face is singing the song.

Our cortex can understand the world because it and the world are both organized hierarchically. Everything in the world is composed of parts that predictably combine to create more complex forms and patterns—molecules into cells into organs into bodies, letters into words into sentences into narratives.

Memory. Such integrated perceptual information is constantly compared to previously related memorized information, and recognition occurs at some point in the processing sequence. It's not necessary for our brain to have all the information before it recognizes something familiar. We can recognize a good friend from the back, from an introductory "Hi" on the phone, or even from a name or number displayed on caller ID.

Most memories involve sequential information, such as a song's melody and lyrics, or a recipe's directions. Our memory represents such complex sequences with a simple identifying title—"America the Beautiful," pecan pie—that can activate the entire sequence. Language thus materially enhances cognitive processing, and narrative ratchets up the process to encompass entire events and sequences of events.

More remarkable, our intelligent brain recognizes and stores information conceptually. For example, although chairs occur in a wide variety of shapes, we can identify an object we've never seen before as a chair (and add it to our memory's *chair* repertoire). This comparison capability sparks analogy and metaphoric thought. As our highly interconnected brain continually seeks matches between what it's currently experiencing and what it has experienced, it activates concepts and specific objects and events that aren't a perfect match but are close enough to be useful. Such metaphoric matches form the base of much of common discourse, fiction, and the arts in general.

For example, many complex novels begin with a simple event that's introduced without context, and the novel then becomes an interpretive expansion of the common metaphor, *it was only the tip of the iceberg*. This introductory literary device is important because intellectual competence requires an understanding that things are often more complicated than they are initially experienced or presented.

The Dr. Seuss (1954) book *Horton Hears a Who!* begins with Horton (an elephant) hearing comments emanating from a floating speck of dust. The speck turns out to be a microscopic community of frightened Whos, who explain their feeling of powerlessness. Horton protects them in a story that explores how the powerful often ignore the plight of the *invisible* powerless and even denounce those who try to help such needy people. Horton believes, however, that "even though you can't see them or hear them at all, a person's a person, no matter how small" (p. 16).

Adults who read the book to children may connect it to various forms of cultural discrimination, and children may connect it to their own relationship with adults. Inserting the exaggerations of a huge fictional animal being concerned about the safety of tiny fictional Whos allows the post-story discussion to focus initially on broader issues of discrimination and abuse rather than on the personal realities that children are currently confronting. Dr. Seuss wrote the book after contemplating political issues surrounding the Japanese shift from a monarchy to a democracy after World War II. Pro-life advocates have used the story as a metaphor for abortion. Fictional narrative thus allows our minds to explore many possibilities that can emerge out of a story in which the beginning is metaphorically only *the tip of the iceberg*.

We live in a complex, ambiguous world, and fictional narratives allow us to mentally explore important concepts and issues before we actually confront them. This is especially true of unusual challenges that pose danger to an individual or relationship, a frequent focus of both childhood and adult fiction. As a child's actual experiences are limited, fictional stories provide a nonthreatening introduction to many issues that will occur in later life. The fictional solution to the challenge also encourages children to think about what's appropriate and inappropriate in such a situation.

Prediction and Intelligence. We've tended to think of cognition as a feed-forward phenomenon, moving from the fragmentary and unknown to the integrated and known to a conscious decision and behavioral response. Hawkins (Hawkins & Blakeslee, 2004) argues, however, that intelligent thought requires the backward flow of information to be as robust as the forward flow. Analysis of cortical organization and the direction of neuronal fiber projections suggest that he's correct.

Hawkins (Hawkins & Blakeslee, 2004) defines intelligence as the ability to rapidly and correctly predict what will occur on the basis of how currently perceived events relate to prior experience (and a child's prior experiences are limited). Prediction requires a continual comparison between what is occurring and what we expect to occur. Feedback pathways can thus insert memories of previous related events and our emotional states related to those events into cognitive processing before sensory input records the actual new event. For example, we expect to see our car in the garage before we actually see it, and a child who breaks an expensive toy anticipates an angry parental response.

We then especially attend to whatever doesn't match our predictions—the car isn't in the garage, the parental response is nurturing. Such unexpected events activate interpretive and problem-solving thoughts and behaviors. An intelligent person with broad experience thus moves confidently through a mostly predictable life, imagining plausible explanations and developing successful alternate strategies when the unexpected occurs.

This supports what most parents and educators do when they provide children with a solid base of information about how the world works in the form of real childhood experiences with nature and society and interesting fabricated stories about what might occur and what to do about it. The resultant knowledge base enhances a successful backward cognitive flow that connects the present challenge with understandings gained from prior real and fictional experiences. The result is that children sometimes respond to a challenge as an adult would—and sometimes they surprise us with a creative response.

CREATIVITY

An intelligent response to a challenge is thus somewhat predictable, in that other intelligent people would have come to the same or a similar decision, or at least we are often not surprised by it. A creative response is much less predictable, and so it's often more interesting.

Nancy Andreasen's (2005) respected research suggests that creativity involves the development of an *original useful product* (assuming broad definitions of the three concepts). *Original* thus doesn't require the product to be entirely new. A creative person can create a new example of an existing form (a symphony or a novel) or a new combination of existing phenomena (putting an engine on a wagon to create an automobile). Similarly, a *useful product* could be the scientific creation of a new medication, but it could also be the strong emotional arousal and extended attention that artistic and literary artifacts prompt.

We can think of creativity in ordinary and extraordinary terms. Ordinary creativity is ubiquitous in that even something as normal as a conversation is incredibly creative. We create conversational comments *on the fly,* shifting thought and syntax at the millisecond level in response to conversational flow and body language. Conversational comments are *original* in that they've typically not been said before, and the informational *product* is typically *useful.*

The results of extraordinary creativity don't typically manifest themselves during childhood, but many of the characteristics of highly creative people can begin to emerge early if appropriately encouraged. Studies of highly creative people indicate that they are intelligent, typically in the 120 to 130 IQ range. They are oriented toward divergent thinking in that they can and prefer to imagine a variety of appropriate responses to a challenge (while convergent thinking involves the search for a single correct answer to a problem).

A highly creative personality thus seeks new experiences, is tolerant of ambiguity, and approaches life and the world relatively free of preconceptions. This flexibility sparks unconventional perceptions that others often don't understand or accept. The highly creative are persistent in expressing their beliefs, however, and so they develop the skills that will allow them to create superior artifacts and explanations that effectively communicate their beliefs.

Creative thinking often moves swiftly and at multiple levels. Solutions often emerge in a flash after a period in which our mind had wandered across the mental landscape that defined the challenge—mentally tagging initially unrelated bits of information.

Children aren't bound by conventional perceptions of phenomena or by established solutions to challenges. Adults tend to see the world in terms of a focused flashlight, while children tend to think in lantern terms—everything is an illuminated possibility. Properly encouraged, children can develop the exploratory tendencies and thought processes that are central to creativity. Limiting them to conventional curricular problems and algorithmic solutions doesn't do much to develop their imaginations and creative potentials. Chapters 2, 5, and 6 discussed the key role of play and games in the development of the exploratory orientation that fosters creativity. The arts provide another powerful, playful venue.

THE ARTS

The real rational world requires an intelligent focus on what actually exists. The imagined world accepts a more creative focus on what might exist. The various forms of the arts thus function within a playful environment that explores multiple responses to every challenge. In the rational world, 6 × 5 = 30 is correct, and everything else is incorrect. The arts beg to differ, with many acceptable solutions to their problems. For example, one of the great appeals of a novel is to discover how it *turns out*, and the ending is typically a surprise to readers.

Artistic expression enters our life very early. Chapter 2 described *Motherese* as the term commonly used for the initial high-pitched, exaggerated, repetitive, melodic communication format that parents use to engage their child's attention. The infant doesn't initially understand the words we use, but simply attends to the verbal and musical communication patterns and rhythms. The joy infants typically express encourages parents to continue Motherese until articulate speech emerges. What's important about this introduction is that children learn best through observing and replicating the behavior of another person, and learning is enhanced when such interactive behavior is aesthetically grounded.

Oral communication thus begins with music, and we often return to music when words alone fail us. Articulate speech provides useful information, but song communicates how we feel about that information, and information without feeling is generally meaningless.

Chapter 2 reported that the planning, regulation, and prediction of movement is a central human property, the principal reason we need a brain. But we not only move, we also seek to move at a virtuoso level—and with style and grace. Chapter 2 suggested that children who get a skateboard will first master basic balance and movement skills, but then they quickly shift their focus to the aesthetics of skateboarding. A skateboard is an ordinary mobility device—four wheels and a board. Adding aesthetics turns skateboarding into a celebration of the ordinary, and that's what the arts do in human life. They turn the ordinary into something extraordinary.

The arts are a win-win phenomenon in that both the doers and observers of artistic activity discover significance in the multiple possibilities that can emerge out of simple exploratory behaviors. How wonderful for children to discover that many stories can emerge from the 26 letters of the alphabet, many melodies can emerge from the 12 tones of the chromatic scale, many drawings can be placed on a sheet of paper, and many objects can be fashioned from a lump of clay.

Perhaps more important, the emotional arousal to an aesthetic challenge activates an attentional focus, and both are prerequisites for understanding and resolving challenges. The arts are thus important because they provide a pleasant, stimulating, interactive venue for developing and maintaining our emotion and attention systems, especially during times when we're not beset by serious challenges. The storyteller and the listeners are both emotionally aroused by and attentive to a good story, as are the musicians and the audience, the painters and those who visit the gallery, and the actors and those who attend the play. Such shared emotion and attention not only helps to maintain key cognitive systems but it also enhances social awareness and development.

Some consider the arts to be educationally important because they supposedly improve math or reading scores or some other culturally important skill. But why should the arts have to justify themselves as a mere adjunct to something else? They've been integral to human life much longer than the multiplication tables and spelling, which evidently don't have to justify their curricular existence.

One could further argue that if it's important for children to learn the sequence of letters that spell a word, it should be equally important to learn the sequence of tones that create a melody, given that song inserts feeling into information. Why would schools seek to develop only the informational and not the affective brain systems that evolved to process communication?

Similarly, precise assessment of the arts is a hopeless enterprise, because the arts can't be narrowly defined, easily measured, or precisely reproduced. Artistic expression is a unique phenomenon. A pianist who plays a concerto with two different orchestras doesn't precisely replicate the first performance even though the notes were identical in both concerts. It's not that musicians play the correct notes, it's *how* they play the notes.

Parents and educators teach basic skills, such as digital competence on musical instruments and computer keyboards, spelling and grammatical skills for writing, mathematical skills for measuring quantity and space, and throwing and jumping skills for sports. Though basic to intelligence and creativity, these skills aren't an end in themselves. They need the nurturing exploratory environment that the reality of nature and the imagination of the arts provide in order to create extraordinary things out of the relatively few simple sequences of symbols and movements that characterize human life. The simple sequential DNA code created the immense variability of the biosphere by simply exploring possible variations over extended time. The exploratory environment of the arts similarly enhances the intellectual and cultural variability that has made humanity what it is.

Home and Beyond Home

From Biology to Technology

Children today may think that radio, TV, computers, video games, the Internet, and cell phones have always existed, but I know that they haven't. For all practical purposes, they emerged during my lifetime. Radio had just arrived as a cultural phenomenon when I was born in 1927, and television followed at about the time my wife and I married at mid-century. Computers, video games, and the Internet achieved widespread use during the last part of the 20th century. Cell phones are basically a 21st-century phenomenon. We're thus at only the beginning of an amazing electronic form of evolution that is already profoundly transforming human interaction.

Writing expanded communication about 6,000 years ago, the printing press expanded writing about 600 years ago, and computers expanded printing about 60 years ago.

The telephone, the first technological expansion of speech, didn't achieve general use until the beginning of the 20th century, and, as indicated above, it took 100 years for cell phones to eliminate the need for telephone wires.

These early technological expansions were somewhat cumbersome, however, so most people considered them a backup system to direct personal conversation, the principal form of interaction throughout human history. Articulate speech provided the efficient communicative system that increasingly complex human societies required. It emerged at least partly out of gesture and music, and its mastery was enhanced by our mirror neuron system. Speech, music, gesture, and imitation are thus central to direct personal interaction.

I have clear childhood recollections of frequent home visits and picnics within our family's friendship circle. The adults discussed personal and cultural issues, and we children played conversation-laced games. Singing around the piano was common. Interactions were personal and direct—so different from the staged discussions now on talk radio and TV.

Credibility is a major problem in communication, so our brain developed what is called a *cheating detector* that can quickly spot lies and deception through the keen observation of subtle variations in body language, eye contact, and intonation. People who haven't developed this skill do poorly at card games. *Faking out* an opponent is an important element in many ball-based games. Although the basics are probably innate, we develop the capability through extended direct experience. The constant interactions in an elementary classroom provide an especially good laboratory for children to master this skill, which may actually be more important over our lifetime than some of the skills measured on state standards tests.

Actors, salesmen, and TV pundits who can successfully control their speech and body language can fool people into believing things that aren't true. The Internet, cable channels, talk radio, and advertising are especially prone to communicating false and deceptive information. This creates challenges for those who must teach children how to differentiate between electronic honesty and deception, and no simple strategy exists so far for that.

It's been fascinating for me to live during this historic transition in interaction, which has gone from direct personal to technologically augmented interaction. Although I fondly recall my conversationally driven childhood, I have no desire to return to its limitations. What's being electronically added to human interaction is quite exciting, even if much of the content is dreadful. As electronic pioneers in a world in which something said anywhere can instantly be heard (and perhaps distorted) everywhere, we'll eventually determine how best to combine direct personal communication with the tremendous capabilities of electronic communication. Like it or not, we're off on a cultural journey with no roadmap (or GPS, for all that) to guide us except for an implicit mandate to do no harm to our children as we try to prepare them for whatever their electronically augmented life will become. Imagine what electronic communication was 10 years ago, and then project what it might be like 10 years from now.

DIRECT AND PERSONAL INTERACTION

We're a social species that now numbers six billion. For most of human history, we lived in relatively small cohesive groups of up to 150 (Gladwell, 2000). This is about the number of people who can become reasonably well acquainted with each other in a stable community. I suspect that most adults have up to 150 acquaintances but fewer than a dozen close friendships. Further, few of our adult friends and acquaintances live within walking distance of each other, as they did in earlier communities.

I have lunch on Tuesdays scheduled with a dozen former colleagues, but the group size on any given Tuesday is typically smaller. I've noticed that if six or fewer attend, a single conversation develops and continues over the lunch, but if the group size is larger than six, two or more independent conversations develop along the extended table. We're cognitively limited in how many people we can directly interact with at a time.

The number of students in an elementary classroom is typically in the 20 to 30 range, and that's also about the size of the school's staff. When a staff gets much larger than that, it's often divided into departments or teams, and meetings become more formal. People who study group dynamics suggest that four to nine is the optimum range for an efficient informal group. It's about the size of most families and childhood playgroups, so we grow up comfortable with it.

Children depend on nurturing adults to teach them how to effectively and appropriately interact with others. Parents begin a child's socialization process within the family and its circle of friends. School adds a more complex situation—non-kin classmates who may have considerably different values.

Chapters 4 to 6 described our 20-year developmental trajectory from childhood dependency to adult autonomy. During childhood, we develop an initial understanding of how the world works, and during adolescence, we begin to develop effective responses to the challenges we confront. We're innately tuned to natural time-space environments, so juveniles adapt to normal time-space challenges with relative ease. Interpersonal relationships typically cause the most problems as juvenile enculturation shifts from family into society.

What's important to add in the context of this chapter is that nurturing adults should provide children with many opportunities for personal nontechnological interaction—to step back a century, as it were, to a simpler time to help children to appreciate and strengthen their innate biological capabilities for direct personal interaction. We shouldn't think in terms of complex activities that require a lot of planning, but rather, we should simply provide intriguing situations that enhance conversation and other forms of direct interaction.

For example, Chapter 7 suggested that although it's often difficult for a family to eat together, it's important to do it and to incorporate a pleasant conversation about what occurred during the day. Family fishing or swimming excursions or going to museums, religious services, and concerts in the park may seem mundane, but these kinds of experiences develop skills in direct human interaction in addition to enhancing family bonds.

It's equally difficult in this era of state-standards pressures for a teacher to find time to periodically take the class for a walk through the neighborhood or to a nearby park, but it's important to do it, and to talk along the way. *Show and tell time* and oral reports are similarly wonderful ways of simply talking to each other about personal interests and experiences. Cooperative-learning activities require more time and effort than individual assignments, but they're important for the development of small-group skills, as is working together to plan and run simple class parties and community projects. If parents and educators don't ground children in our basic social identity in an increasingly electronic culture, who will?

ELECTRONICALLY AUGMENTED INTERACTION

Invention occurs when conditions encourage or require it. The gradual multimillennial move from speech to cell phones was thus probably inevitable as our creative brain confronted the increased complexity of communication within a growing and increasingly mobile global population. The recent technological escalation suggests that we now also live in a parallel cyber time-space environment that differs substantially from our natural time-space environment, and especially in our information-gathering and communicative capabilities and systems.

Prensky (2009) suggests that our culture is now made up of digital natives and digital immigrants. Digital natives are those who were born or went through their juvenile years during this recent electronic escalation. They easily master the new interactive technologies through play and games just as the older generations mastered natural time-space through play and games. Digital natives comfortably multitask on a computer screen just as they easily learned to observe and respond to a variety of foreground and background activity in soccer and other games they play. Cell phones and computers increasingly mediate their social interactions.

Digital immigrants are those of us who came into this new environment later in life. Our brain had been tuned to the rhythms and complexities of natural time-space, and so we tend to respond to challenges one by one and step by step. Our social life focuses on direct interaction with friends and business contacts. We study the printed manuals of all new technologies we acquire, much like we read descriptive print materials about places we intend to visit.

It took me a long time to move from thinking of my first computer as a really expensive typewriter to the ease I now have with it as a transformative device. And then, I had to start all over again with cell phones and other portable technologies. So, older folks are like immigrants to a new country and its culture. We begin with the elements we can easily master and avoid or seek help for those we can't. For example, my wife and I prefer the feel and format of a daily newspaper, but our grandchildren tend to get their news via the Internet.

The reality is that all of us now live in both environments, and it's a potentially wonderful win-win situation. Digital natives and immigrants can both benefit from the knowledge and skills we honed in our respective juvenile years if we both can meld them into our current more complex parallel environments.

Think of how much richer our culture is because of all the traditions, foods, crafts, music, and other elements that immigrants have transported from foreign cultures into our culture. Digital natives and immigrants bring different but important knowledge and skills to the melding task. What digital immigrants can do best is to help digital natives develop and use interpersonal skills in face-to-face situations, skills that are at risk when communication becomes increasingly electronic. What digital natives can do is to help digital immigrants master the new technologies. I suspect that much of this already occurs as children and grandchildren solve the technological glitches that mystify their elders, and their elders help them solve the kinds of real-life problems that aren't incorporated into video games or Internet sources. The number of digital natives is increasing and the number of digital immigrants is decreasing as computerized technologies expand into more areas of human life.

Cyber Worlds and the "Real" World

Last week, an elementary-age grandson posted a short animated film he had developed on YouTube. I was simply amazed, but the truth is that he's not the only elementary student who has recently done something like this. It does, however, raise the important issue of what's developmentally appropriate for children who must master the challenges of both natural time-space and cyber time-space, but are perhaps more interested in cyber environments than in natural environments. Let's explore that issue.

The conventional wisdom is that extensive interactions with electronic media provoke culturally inappropriate behavior and reduce problem-solving abilities, that they *dumb down society*, as it were. An analysis of credible research on this issue suggests the opposite (Johnson, 2005). Although the entire human age range uses electronic media, their use begins during childhood, so it's important in the context of this book to examine what is known about them and their effects.

The principal criticisms of electronic media focus on their content rather than on the cognitive demands they make on those who use them. Further, many of the critics have little first-hand knowledge about the current nature of the formats they criticize, and they tend to overestimate the amount of violent and sexual content.

Popular culture is not high culture, and so it shouldn't be compared to it. Folks typically don't play video games or watch popular TV programs to broaden their intellectual horizons. Those who golf, fish, solve crossword puzzles, or play cards similarly don't do it to materially enhance their intellect. What all such activities have in common is that they increase knowledge and/or problem-solving abilities within specific parameters of interest to the players.

For example, book reading is an activity that critics of electronic media consider more intellectually stimulating than video games, but it's basically the passive observation of someone else's thought processes. The reader tries to predict what will occur in a novel, but has no control over the narrative flow, and this is also the case with those who observe TV shows and films.

Video Games

Conversely, a person who is playing a complex contemporary video game must first determine the purpose and rules of the game (which typically aren't provided) and then continually make decisions that can actually alter the course of the game, always with the basic presumed goal of the game in mind. The content of such video games is thus secondary to the thought processes involved in planning and executing strategies and in predicting the movements of the video game and one's opponents. The same things would be true of a chess or tennis match or even of fishing.

Most games (including video games) aren't really pleasurable when complex challenges loom—such as third and long in football or the loss of a queen in chess. But, such situations get the juices flowing in players who seek challenge within the game. Players must quickly and successfully draw on related previous strategies, or they must make creative risky decisions in order to stay in the game, and this enhances their problem-solving abilities within that setting.

A game must thus have a strong emotional attraction that will maintain the effort the game requires. Competition, violence, and sexuality are innately arousing emotionally, and so it's not surprising that they're explicit (or at least implicit) in many games and media narratives. Indeed, even revered childhood fairy tales contain violent and sexual themes. Hansel and Gretel worried about getting baked in an oven, and a princess kissed a frog in "The Frog Prince." How kinky can a children's fairy tale get?

The challenge and complexity of the most popular newer video games are such that they don't need a heavy dose of violence and sexuality to initiate and maintain interest. For example, the popular *SimCity* series of games challenges the player to design a complex metropolis, and the continually popular *Tetris* forces the player to quickly make decisions about the placement of geometric shapes.

Video games (and other games, such as hockey and football) that require aggressive responses to dangerous situations will obviously strengthen the neural circuitry that processes similar decisions. It's problematic, though, whether this increased capability makes the player more aggressive generally in the real world. Current commentary on this issue is based more on opinion than solid research. It's very difficult to do credible cause-and-effect research on this issue.

I suspect that many folks who decry the violence and sexuality that they believe is endemic in video games watch TV shows and sports that contain violent and sexual content, and are oblivious to the inconsistency between their beliefs and behavior.

Many current video games allow players who live apart to collaborate and compete in a game, and this suggests that this technological development may eventually enhance our ability to interact at a new personal level via computers—to develop an electronic capability that's analogous to our biological cheating detector.

TV and Film

Like readers, viewers of projected media don't control or even affect the narrative flow. They will often guess the answers in TV quiz shows, critique the flow of reality shows and contests, call in to talk shows, and discuss the shows and films they've seen, but TV and films are much more passive than video games. We sit forward for video games and sit back for TV and films.

We should thus differentiate between intelligent TV shows and films and those that force us to be intelligent.

Intelligent productions go beyond clichés and provide stimulating plots and witty dialogue. The basic intelligence portrayed exists within the people on the screen, however, and not within the viewers.

Conversely, the plots and subplots of many contemporary fictional TV shows and films are complex and convoluted, omit plot information that the viewer must insert, don't clearly differentiate between foreground and background, and require knowledge of areas such as law and medicine that goes beyond the conventional. Such programs make real intellectual demands on viewers, and that enhances their appeal. This trend toward intellectual complexity has also emerged in TV shows and films that appeal to juveniles, and it's a trend that will certainly continue. The reality is that all forms of print and projected media run the gamut from the schlocky to the scholarly.

Mass media tend to focus on the unusual because our brain automatically attends to anything that differs from what's normal or expected, and getting and maintaining attention is crucial for media that depend on advertising revenue. We're thus not much interested in an evening news broadcast that informs us that most people went to lunch over the noon hour, but we will attend to segments that describe new community developments, violent acts, and unusual acts of kindness.

At issue, then, is not so much what television or other forms of mass media bring to a child, but rather what the child brings to the media programming. Children who live in a secure home and school environment in which adults model positive human behavior will interpret socially negative content for what it is—a report on an abnormal event or a fictional narrative that describes something unusual that might occur. Nurturing adults will help them understand the context and suggest how to respond if such depicted events ever occur. Conversely, children who live in a socially negative environment are more apt to think that the violence and immorality they experience in real life are normal, as they're also depicted on TV. And unfortunately, the adults in their lives often can't provide an appropriate context for what the children observed on TV or experience in real life.

The Internet

The networking that permeates the Internet makes it potentially the most intellectually challenging of the new media forms, and probably also the most developmentally dangerous, given that a rite of passage for many first graders now is to get an e-mail address. Consider what e-mail, websites, and search engines could do a few years ago and what they can do now. For example, social networking systems and blogs have developed during the past five years, and cell phones have now become cameras that connect to the Internet. Project ahead five years, and it's obvious that many new interactive forms will emerge that will force sophisticated thought.

Young people tend to depend on their peers to teach them how to use the new electronic technologies because the adults in their life typically don't understand the mechanics. What adults can and should do is to teach children appropriate behavior, something their peers typically lack the judgment to do.

Print media are expensive and so publishers typically check sources to insure credibility. A student who cites a print source in a course paper is thus more certain of its credibility than a student who clips information off a website. The Internet is an informational free-for-all, and so sexual predators, con artists, and folks who want to spread misinformation can do it as easily as those who act responsibly. It takes intelligence to stay one step ahead of Internet trash and treachery. Our cheating detector, which works so well in face-to-face interaction, doesn't work with unseen correspondents who can easily pretend to be someone else. A major task of the school will thus be to teach students how to assess credibility on the Internet, and this process should begin during the elementary school years.

Wikipedia and similar resources are simply wonderful in their currency and immediate accessibility, but they certainly aren't the *Encyclopaedia Britannica* in terms of credibility.

The recent development of e-books (such as the Kindle) may well revolutionize publishing and further reduce our need for paper. This is a trend that began with e-mail, which has almost eliminated personal surface mail. The e-book equipment price will go down to the point where it will become cheaper to provide students with e-books instead of textbooks. Electronic publishing means that science textbooks, for example, can be frequently revised as new discoveries occur. Soon, newspapers and magazines may well only publish electronically. Will bookstores and libraries disappear, or will they redesign themselves?

Pac-Man and Donkey Kong almost defined the video game genre a half-generation ago, and other forms of electronic media have similarly exploded within our culture. We won't return to what was. The challenge for parents and educators is to prepare the next generation for the natural and electronic environments in which they will live. The challenge isn't as hopeless as it seems. The electronic media developments that many consider to be culturally negative may actually be intellectually positive.

Texting is changing spelling, just as the ease of editing implicit in computer software changed the way writers develop manuscripts. Children now spend an incredible amount of energy in mastering technologies that didn't even exist when they were born. How wonderful (and somewhat frightening) to be at the edge of such an amazing cultural transformation!

Preparing for Adolescence

From a Sheltered Childhood Toward an
Autonomous Adulthood

It comes down this: A fetus becomes an infant becomes a child becomes an adolescent becomes an autonomous adult. Each developmental stage has its own individual integrity, but it should also provide a smooth transition into the next stage. This book is focused on childhood, but it should also explore the transition into adolescence.

PARALLEL ENVIRONMENTS

The principal task of childhood is to discover how the world works. The world of 21st-century children is far more complex than that of their forebears: It now encompasses parallel natural and electronic environments and the cultural issues that emerge out of them. Most adults are reasonably informed about the basics of our natural environment, and so they can introduce them to children, but many adults have a limited understanding of the recent biological and electronic developments that will play increasingly important roles in the adolescent and adult lives of 21st-century children.

This limited understanding thus becomes an important issue for parents and educators who must guide a child's introduction into such developments. This book has argued that the best way for juveniles to begin the mastery of anything is to simply *play* with it, to explore what it can and can't do and then to seek any needed further information from those who have it. Most adults similarly need only a functional (rather than a technical) understanding of many phenomena that affect our lives, and if we need more than that, we call a plumber or go to a physician. This book provides the basic functional information that adults need in order to understand child cognition and to help children begin to understand their own cognitive processes.

We can think of many of the emerging electronic technologies as an external layer of brain tissue, as they process functions that our brain also processes. They communicate with others, gather and remember information, calculate quantities, and process other tasks that our brain can't do at all or can't do very effectively. For example, we developed neuroimaging technologies because we can't see through skin and skull. We developed cell phones to contact people who might not be near a regular phone connection. When adults draw functional parallels between brain systems and related electronic technologies that children play with, it provides an understandable introduction to both phenomena that children can then expand during adolescence and adulthood.

Movement in all of its wondrous manifestations is our brain's defining property. Adults should thus similarly draw parallels between a child's movement activities and the cognitive processes that regulate them. Adolescent movement becomes more skilled and consciously goal directed, so it's important for children to develop basic movement skills and an initial functional sense of the biological dynamics and cultural conventions of movement.

Brain Dichotomies

The concept of dichotomy is central to a functional understanding of our brain and its systems. At the neuronal level, a neuron either fires or doesn't fire. At the brain systems level, we're emotionally aroused or not aroused by a stimulus, we attend or don't attend to an object or event, we respond or don't respond to a challenge. Functionally, our brain is simply a collaborating set of dichotomous systems that recognize and respond to novel and familiar dangers and opportunities that we confront in our natural and electronic space-time environments.

Further, our brain's development follows a trajectory defined by a childhood-adolescence dichotomy. As indicated above and in Chapter 4, childhood focuses on understanding how the world works, and adolescence focuses on determining how best to respond to the challenges we confront.

The world a child seeks to understand has considerable factual precision. If we throw something up, it will come down. A maple tree sheds its leaves during autumn. Fish live in the water. We can thus think of the child's exploratory world as pretty much a true-false dichotomy with a lot of built-in predictability. And when children get to school, they discover that $6 \times 5 = 30$, and dog is spelled d-o-g.

The adolescent and adult worlds that children are moving toward are more ambiguous. Mature people consider alternatives, have preferences, and make choices about the challenges they confront. Their problem-solving dichotomies aren't principally about factual true-false propositions (such as $6 \times 5 = 30$) but depend more on judgment—right/wrong, good/bad, fair/unfair, and successful/unsuccessful. Think of a restaurant menu that contains a lot of factual information about ingredients and prices, but the essence of a menu is that it contains no single correct response. Four people seated at a table can order completely different meals that represent their individual preferences.

Children obviously have preferences and make decisions about many things, but adults make most of the important decisions, and they monitor and frequently override the decisions that children do make. Children are compliant about this for the most part because they're so dependent on adults. *Don't bite the hand that feeds you* is thus probably an innate aphorism even if children often fuss about adult requests and decisions. Children should become more involved in decisions about their lives as they approach adolescence. The simplest way for adults to begin the process is to explain the reasons for the decisions they make.

Nurturing adults should thus help children understand the difference between the concept of *facts,* which are central to a child's understanding of how the world works, and *beliefs,* which become increasingly important during the adolescent move toward autonomy.

A Social Species

We're a social species, highly dependent on each other, and children are absolutely dependent on nurturing adults. The neurobiology of bonding, mirror neurons, and various language and other communicative skills make social interaction possible.

Adolescence marks the beginning of the periodically acrimonious journey toward adult autonomy. It's important that children develop the kind of positive relationships to the adults in their lives that will enhance their later relationships. If the significant adults in their lives unconditionally love them—loving them for who they are rather than how they behave—it will certainly help smooth over any rough edges that will develop during adolescence and adulthood. More important, it provides wonderful modeling for the social relationships adolescents and adults develop.

We live in a democratic society, so it's important that children develop an understanding of and experience with its underlying principles. Chapter 6 suggested a classroom-management model that introduces children to democratic values and procedures, and it also encouraged a democratic family perspective in which adults and juveniles collaborate in family decisions and tasks.

AN EXTENDED DEVELOPMENT

Our extended maturation means that juveniles can develop personal interests and capabilities at a relaxed pace, but it also means that children are expected to master culturally but not personally important information and skills (such as state capitals and multiplication tables). People who live in developed societies spend almost one-third of their lives in mastering the complexities of their culture and of other related cultures before they become independent, and this allows them to also think beyond their family's cultural and vocational perspective. The increased global connectivity made possible by electronic media adds importance to a childhood introduction to the basics of the universality and differentiation of human life.

THE ARTS

We now live in parallel natural and electronic environments, but humans have always lived in parallel factual and fictional environments. Chapter 10 introduced this concept, and it's probably appropriate to end this book with how important it is for children to become grounded in the alternate reality of the arts. A renowned pianist was once asked to explain the difference between a piano player and a pianist. He responded, "Anyone can play the correct notes." An important part of playing the piano involves factual elements—for example, pressing down on the keys. But it's *how* we press down on the keys that introduces aesthetics into playing the piano.

Children should be introduced to such factual elements of the arts because (like language) they can easily master the mechanics of musical instruments, dancing, and other art forms during childhood. Similarly, the childhood understanding and mastery of the regularities implicit in the multiplication tables is a prerequisite to an adult mastery of mathematics, but mathematics certainly involves much more than computation. To view elementary education as focused only on the true-false mechanical prerequisites of a cognitive field is a very limited perspective of what childhood is all about.

Children do need to learn how to spell and how to mix papier-mâché, but they also need to learn how to soar creatively. Fictional narrative soars in its invention of an imagined world, and so do the rest of the arts.

Adults developed the wonderfully powerful portable computers that are revolutionizing cultural interaction, but juveniles who had been taught the precision of spelling developed the creative alternate spelling and texting forms that now drive the system.

An elementary education bereft of the arts thus isn't an appropriate 21st-century education. It sells childhood short, and it doesn't provide a responsible transition into a productive mature life.

On one level, life would be much simpler if 10 or so magic rules for parenting and teaching existed. Adults could then apply the rules and infancy would merge seamlessly into childhood, which would merge seamlessly into adolescence, which would merge seamlessly into a successful autonomous adulthood. It doesn't work that way. If it did, the adult nurturing of juveniles would be boring. I wrote in the introduction that I'm a father and grandfather to a couple dozen, and I've been a teacher to many thousands. The young people I nurtured were both similar and different. Their similarities meant that I didn't have to start from scratch with each nurturing task, and their differences meant that my personal and professional challenges have been very stimulating, albeit often frustrating.

It would also have been helpful on many occasions if I knew then what I know now, but again, how boring my life would have been if I didn't have to learn anything new along the way. I've thus tried to write in this book what I've learned about childhood and its nurturing from personal experience and professional study, but all I could honestly do was to provide you with useful background knowledge and a general guideline for resolving the challenges you will confront.

That's what I got at mid-20th century when I began to nurture my own and other children, and that guideline was based on what we knew then about childhood. A child's brain has remained biologically constant in the intervening years, except that we now know much more about it, and this book provides the core of that information. Conversely, the cultural and technological context in which a childhood brain matures has changed considerably during my lifetime, and it will continue to escalate in the foreseeable future. The good news is that humans have achieved biological success over the millennia because of their ability to adapt to new challenges.

So, my advice is to go forth with what you've learned in confident optimism—and with a lot of underlying unconditional love. Good luck!

Glossary

Amino Acids. Molecules that are the chemical building blocks of proteins and neurotransmitters. Four types of molecules provide the construction base of all organisms: amino acids, fatty acids, nucleotides, and sugars.

Angular Gyrus. A hemispheric region located at the juncture of the occipital, parietal, and temporal lobes. Among other things, it connects the various elements of language comprehension and metaphoric understanding.

Anterior Commissure. A connecting pathway (below and in front of the corpus callosum) that exchanges emotional information between the two cerebral hemispheres.

Axon. The tubular extension of a neuron that transmits information from the neuron cell body to other neurons. See Appendix A for additional information.

Brainstem. The finger-size structure at the base of the brain that regulates such survival functions as circulation, respiration, and endocrine gland activity. It also transmits sensorimotor information between the body and brain.

Caudate Nucleus. An important element of the brain's movement, pleasure, and reward circuitry. It's located deep within the brain.

Cerebellum. A two-hemisphere structure located behind the brainstem, tucked under the cerebral hemispheres. It plays important roles in planning and executing behaviors, including the smooth regulation of such automatic movements as walking.

Cerebrum. The large upper two-hemisphere section of the brain that processes conscious activity. It includes the top, deeply folded cerebral cortex layer of cells (gray matter) and its underlying network of axons that connect neurons and networks (white matter).

Cingulate. A processing system located above the corpus callosum that integrates information from many brain areas in the resolution of ambiguous challenges.

Corpus Callosum. A connective band of more than 200 million myelinated axons that exchanges conscious thought between the two cerebral hemispheres.

Cortex. The large, deeply folded top layer of our brain that processes thought and action.

Dendrites. The large number of short tubular extensions from a neuronal cell body that receive molecular (neurotransmitter) information from the axons of other neurons. See Appendix A for additional information.

DNA (deoxyribonucleic acid). A ladder-shaped, meter-long, twisted and folded, self-replicating molecule that forms much of a cell's nucleus. All cells within an organism except egg, sperm, and red blood cells have identical DNA molecules. DNA provides the genetic instructions for constructing and maintaining an organism, and it also transmits genetic information to an organism's subsequent generations.

Dopamine. A neurotransmitter that helps to regulate emotional behaviors and conscious movements.

Ectoderm. The embryonic tissue that forms the surface of the embryo and, eventually, the skin and central nervous system.

Emotion. An unconscious arousal system that alerts the rest of our brain to potential dangers and opportunities.

Endorphin. A class of neurotransmitters, chemically related to opium and morphine, that reduce pain and enhance euphoria.

Estrogen. A hormone that plays an important regulatory role in the female reproductive cycle and behavior. Males also have estrogen, but at much lower levels.

Frontal Lobes. The front sections of the two cerebral hemispheres that play the central role in solving problems and initiating responsive actions.

Gene. A segment of DNA that contains the coded directions for assembling a protein molecule out of a unique sequence of the 20 different kinds of amino acids.

Glial Support Cells. The perhaps trillion brain cells that provide a variety of support services for neurons. They are much smaller than neurons but make up about half the mass of our brain. See Appendix A for additional information.

Gray Matter. See Gray and White Matter.

Gray and White Matter. Gray matter is the aggregate of cellular columns that extend vertically through the six layers of the cerebral cortex. Individual columns and related sets of columns process a specific units of information, such as to respond to vertical lines or to activate a muscle. The underlying white matter is the dense web of axons that connect columns to each other and to muscles and sense organs. The term *gray matter* comes from the gray color of preserved neuronal cell bodies. Because the myelin sheath that covers an axon is white, the underlying axonal web is called the *white matter.*

Hypothalamus. A structure in the center of the brain that directly and indirectly regulates most body functions. It's often called the *brain's brain.*

Insula. Two thumb-sized, pyramid-shaped structures deep within the folds of the two cerebral hemispheres that help process several important functions, such as feeling pain, processing taste, translating unconscious emotions into conscious feelings, and sequencing speech movements.

Limbic System. An ill-defined ring of interconnected cortical and subcortical structures that surround the brainstem. It was long thought to regulate emotional activity and memory, but that view is changing as scientists develop a better understanding of these processes.

Locus Coeruleus. A brainstem system that secretes the neurotransmitter norepinephrine and plays a central role in attentional focus and response to stressful situations.

Lymphatic System. A system of organs, ducts, and nodes that transports the lymph fluid that distributes immune cells and other elements throughout the body and assists the circulatory system in delivering nutrients to and removing waste from body tissues.

Microbes. A form of life that's typically invisible to humans, and includes protozoa, bacteria, and fungi.

Mirror Neurons. A class of neurons that primes voluntary movements but that also activates when we see someone else carry out the same behavior. They are the neural substrate of mimicry.

Motor Cortex. A two-inch wide band of cortical columns that initiates conscious movements. It stretches across our brain from ear to ear, with specific areas devoted to the various parts of our motor system.

Myelin. Glial cells that wrap around long neuronal axons to create an insulating layer that increases the efficiency of neuronal transmission. See Appendix A for additional information.

Neural network. A set or circuit of neurons joined together to carry out a specific function.

Neuroimaging Technologies. Recently developed computerized machines that measure and display the variations in chemical composition, blood flow patterns, and electromagnetic fields that occur in normal and abnormal brains. Researchers use these technologies to diagnose illness and to interpret behavior.

Neuron. A specialized cell that transmits information within a brain and between the brain and body. Neurons have many short dendritic extensions, which receive information from other neurons and sensorimotor systems, and a (typically single) longer axon extension that sends information to other neurons and sensorimotor systems. See Appendix A for additional information.

Neurotransmitter. One of 50-plus different kinds of molecules that transmit chemical information within our central and peripheral nervous systems. See Appendix A for additional information.

Norepinephrine. The principal neurotransmitter for regulating blood pressure and activating stress-related responses. It's also called noradrenaline.

Nucleus Accumbens. A structure within the dopamine circuitry that is associated with pleasure and reward and is strongly implicated in addiction.

Occipital Lobes. Paired sensory lobes in the upper rear section of the cerebral cortex that process vision and related phenomena.

Olfactory Bulb. A key part of the olfactory (smell) system. It's a bulb-shaped enlargement of the end of the olfactory nerve, located above the nasal cavity and underneath the frontal lobes.

Organ Systems. The human body has several organ systems: *circulatory* (cardiovascular: heart, blood; lymphatic: lymph nodes and vessels, thymus, spleen), *digestive* (primary organs: mouth, stomach, intestines, rectum; secondary organs: teeth, tongue, liver, pancreas), *endocrine* (pituitary gland, pineal gland, ovaries, testes, thyroid gland), *integumentary* or "barrier" system (skin, nails, hair, sweat glands), *muscular* (muscles), *nervous* (brain, spinal cord, nerves), *respiratory* (nose, lungs, trachea, bronchi), *reproductive* (male: testes, scrotum, penis, vas deferens, prostate; female: ovaries, uterus, vagina, mammary glands), *skeletal* (bones, joints), *urinary,* and *excretory* (kidneys, urinary bladder, urethra, ureters).

Oxytocin. A pituitary hormone that initiates the uterine contractions in childbirth and lactation in breast-feeding. It also enhances social and bonding behaviors in both males and females.

Parietal Lobes. Paired sensory lobes in the upper back section of our cerebral cortex that process touch sensations, body and joint orientation, and space/location relationships.

Pheromones. Hormone-like molecules that travel via the air or through physical contact to transmit strong social or sexual messages within a species.

Plasticity. The ability of neurons and neuronal networks to change their properties, organization, and/or function through new experiences. To do this, they alter existing axon/dendrite extensions, create new synapses, and/or change the strength of existing synapses.

Premotor Area. The front (anterior) part of the motor cortex where mirror neurons prime conscious movement sequences.

Protein. Organic compounds made up of specific genetic sequences of amino acids (genes) that are arranged linearly but folded into a globular form. Proteins are the chief building blocks of cells and tissues.

RNA (ribonucleic acid). A molecule that's central to the synthesis of proteins. Think of the cell as a kitchen, DNA as the recipe for a protein, and RNA as the cook who reads the DNA recipe, and then assembles it from the nutrient materials within the cellular cytoplasm.

Septum. One of several systems that process feelings of pleasure.

Serotonin. A neurotransmitter that inhibits awkward and impulsive movements and so enhances smooth fluid movements. Since movement is a central human property, elevated serotonin levels are associated with high self-esteem (and vice versa).

Stem Cells. Immature cells that initially can reproduce and develop into any type of body or brain cell—typically, into the kind of cells prevalent in the area where the stem cell is located.

Sub Cortical Area. All brain tissue and systems that are located beneath the cerebral cortex.

Temporal Lobes. Paired sensory lobes on the back and side of the cerebral cortex that process hearing, smell, taste, language and music perception, complex visual processing (such as face recognition), and memory.

Testosterone. A hormone associated principally with male reproductive behavior and with the escalation of aggressive male and female behavior.

Thalamus. A key initial relay station deep within the cerebral cortex that processes all the senses except the sense of smell.

Vasopressin. A hormone that helps to regulate water retention and blood pressure and that enhances male and female social and bonding behaviors.

White Matter. See Gray and White Matter.

Appendix A

Neurons and Glial Cells

NEURONS

Humans have an estimated 100 billion neurons organized into complex networks. An average human head has 10,000 hairs, so one human has as many neurons as the amount of hair in a population of 10 million people (such as metropolitan New York City). A neuron can directly interact with thousands of other cells, so the molecular information in a neuron is only a few neurons away from any other neuron. If you think this implausible, consider the one billion telephones in the world and the relatively simple coding system of up to a dozen digits that can rapidly connect any two phones.

A neuron's cell body contains all the structures that maintain cellular functions. An individual neuron can remain functional throughout our lifetime, but it rebuilds itself every three months or so, molecule by molecule, as parts wear out. The cell body and its DNA genetic system use the nutrients from the circulatory system to maintain the cell and to synthesize the neurotransmitter molecules that are central to its communications with other cells.

The typical neuron cell body contains many short, finger-like, tubular extensions, called dendrites, that receive information from other neurons. Dendrites can extend a millimeter or so into the surrounding area, which doesn't seem like much until you realize how densely packed neurons are. Dendrites contain many receptors, protein molecules that extend through the dendrite's membrane to receive chemical messages carried by another neuron's neurotransmitter molecules. Spines may develop on dendrites during memory formation, increasing the number of receptors and therefore the amount of neurotransmitter information that can enter the neuron at one time.

A typical neuron also has an axon extension that sends the neuron's message to other neurons in the circuit. Motor neuron axons, which extend from the brain to muscles, can be a meter or more in length, but most axons are in the millimeter range. The axon may divide into branches toward its end and thus send its message to many other cells. The ending of an axon is called a terminal or bouton, and it is here that a neuron stores its neurotransmitters in little packets called vesicles while they wait to be released.

Neuronal Transmission. Neuron cell bodies and their many dendrite extensions constantly receive various levels of excitatory (send) and inhibitory (don't send) information from related neurons. This information is averaged within the cell body, and if it reaches the neuron's firing threshold (send) at a given moment, an action potential develops and the message rapidly moves along the axon to the terminal in a process called depolarization. This movement of a neural message along an axon has been likened to an electrical charge. It does have some similarities, but neural messages don't move in the same way that electrical currents do. It's also more complicated biochemically than the following brief functional explanation.

The inside of an axon has a slight negative charge, and the cellular fluids outside the axon have a slight positive charge. When a neuron reaches its firing threshold, it propagates a signal down the axon that rapidly opens and closes a series of channels (pores in the axon membrane through which electrically charged ions can pass). When a set of depolarized channels opens, positively charged sodium ions from the fluids outside the neuron enter the axon. This action briefly changes the charge inside that part of the axon from negative to positive, and this also triggers the opening of the next set of channels. The process is then repeated with the next set of channels. Think of a row of dominoes falling over. Each domino pushes the next one just as each set of channels opens the next set.

After a set of channels opens, the sodium ions are pumped out, the channels close, and that part of the axon once again has a negative charge—until the next axon potential propagates down the axon.

When the axon's wave of permeability to sodium ions (the sequential opening and closing of channels) reaches the axon terminal, calcium ions enter the terminal, triggering the release of packets (vesicles) of neurotransmitters into the synapse, a very narrow gap between the axon of one neuron and the dendrite of another. The neurotransmitters attach to the appropriate receptors in the dendrites and/or cell body of the postsynaptic neuron, and thereby pass their neuron's molecular message on to the next neuron. Most neurotransmitters then return to the terminal via reuptake channels for reuse in subsequent action potentials.

Glial Cells

Glial cells constitute a vast support system for neurons. Our brain has 10 times as many glial cells as neurons, and they comprise about half of the mass of our brain.

Although glial cells do not transmit the same kind of cognitive information neurons transmit, recent discoveries suggest that they use chemical signals to affect both the synaptic communication among neurons and the formation of synapses. They thus play a far more significant role in learning and memory than formerly thought.

Glia means glue, and glial cells were originally thought to be the glue that holds our brain together. In fetal brain development, star-shaped glial cells called astrocytes do act as a scaffolding of sorts that newly formed cerebral cortex neurons use in migrating from the subcortical region where they were created to the specific site in a cortical column and layer where they will carry out their appropriate neuronal function. Glial cells thus play a key role in establishing the general architecture of our brain. Chapter 4 suggested that glial cell extensions can be thought of as the scaffolding of a *cortical* building, and the six layers of neurons that comprise the cortex can be thought of as the floors, walls, furniture, and so forth that are then attached to the scaffolding during construction.

Our brain must tightly control the chemical balance within its cells because chemical imbalances can result in mental illness. Glial astrocyte cells assist in this task by forming part of the blood-brain barrier that surrounds the capillaries, thus denying entry into our brain to many unnecessary or dangerous molecules that travel in the bloodstream.

Another type of glial cells, called oligodendrocytes, form an insulating layer called myelin around nerve fibers (axons) that send messages to distant cells, and this insulation increases the speed and precision of such neural messages. Multiple sclerosis is a disease that results from the deterioration of the myelin sheath.

Microglia are small glial cells that proliferate in response to injury in order to absorb damaged cells and any foreign bodies in the area. They thus serve a sort of immune system function.

Glial cells located in the peripheral nervous system have different names but similar functions. Schwann cells, like oligodendrocytes, create the myelin in peripheral neurons that surrounds both the axons and the synapses where the axon terminal and muscle meet. Satellite cells serve the same protective role as the microglia.

Appendix B

Theories of Multiple Intelligences

Educators embraced the concept of multiple intelligences because it relates well to the way formal education is organized. Several theories have emerged, but Howard Gardner's theory of multiple intelligences is probably the best-known theory in educational circles. Critics of MI theory (as it is commonly called) suggest that the *intelligences* suggested by the various MI categories aren't intelligences but are rather specific cognitive capabilities that correlate variously with a person's general intelligence (or IQ). As indicated in Chapter 10, the three principal MI theorists are Howard Gardner, Robert Sternberg, and David Perkins.

Howard Gardner currently proposes eight forms of intelligence that focus on one's ability to successfully process key identity, space, and time elements of human life. He labels them in noun terms: *Intrapersonal* and *interpersonal* intelligences reflect one's capabilities with the personal and social elements of information and problems. *Spatial, bodily-kinesthetic,* and *naturalist* intelligences reflect one's capabilities with the space/place elements of information and problems. *Language, musical,* and *logical-mathematical* intelligences reflect one's capabilities with temporal/sequential information and elements of problems (for example, *dog* and *god* have the same letters but in different sequences).

Robert Sternberg proposed a triarchic theory of intelligence that labels its elements in verb terms. *Creative intelligence* involves the cognitive processes that identify and formulate good problems and ideas, question existing assumptions, and overcome obstacles in developing new ways to do things. *Analytic intelligence* involves the cognitive processes that consciously solve well- or ill-structured problems, make intuitive and reasoned decisions among choices, and judge the quality of ideas. *Practical intelligence* involves the action-oriented cognitive processes developed principally through experience that help us to effectively analyze challenges confronted in everyday life and then to use this information to solve such problems—the term *street smarts* comes to mind.

David Perkins views intelligence as distributed within our brain and culture through various human and machine interactions, affected by the cognitive overload of our complex culture, dialectic in its multiple approaches to problems, and metacognitive in its self-awareness of its own cognitive behavior. Perkins sees intelligence as encompassing three elements: *Neural intelligence* involves the quantity, quality, speed, and precision of our various innate brain systems. *Experiential intelligence* involves specialized early and useful context-specific experiences. And *reflective intelligence* involves reflective regulation of our knowledge, skills, and attitudes—in effect, knowing *our way around* various knowledge and skill realms that define human life.

Print and Electronic References and Additional Resources

PRINT REFERENCES AND RESOURCES

Ackerman, D. (2004). *An alchemy of mind: The marvel and mystery of the brain.* New York: Scribners.

Andreasen, N. (2005). *The creating brain: The neuroscience of genius.* New York: Dana Press.

Blakeslee, S. (2006, January 10). Cells that read minds. *The New York Times.* Retrieved May 6, 2010, from http://www.nytimes.com/2006/01/10/science/10mirr.html?_r=1&scp=1&sq=cells%20that%20read%20minds&st=cse.

Blakeslee, S., & Blakeslee, M. (2007). *The body has a mind of its own: How body maps in your brain help you to do (almost) everything better.* New York: Random House.

Boyd, B. (2009). *On the origin of stories: Evolution, cognition, and fiction.* Cambridge, MA: Belknap/Harvard Press.

Brown, S. (2009). *Play: How it shapes the brain, opens the imagination, and invigorates the soul.* New York: Avery.

Caine, R., Caine, G., McClintic, C., & Klimek K. (2005). *12 brain/mind learning principles in action.* Thousand Oaks, CA: Corwin.

Corballis, M. (2002). *From hand to mouth: The origins of language.* Princeton, NJ: Princeton University Press.

Damasio, A. (2003). *Looking for Spinoza: Joy, sorrow, and the feeling brain.* New York: Harcourt Brace.

Dewey, J. (1916). *Democracy and education: An introduction to the philosophy of education.* New York: Macmillan.

Dissanayake, E. (2000). *Art and intimacy: How the arts began.* Seattle: University of Washington Press.

Fogarty, R. (2009). *Brain-compatible classrooms* (3rd ed.). Thousand Oaks, CA: Corwin.

Gardner, H. (1983). *Frames of mind: The theory of multiple intelligences.* New York: Basic Books.

Gladwell, M. (2000). *The tipping point—How little things make a big difference.* New York: Little, Brown and Company.

Gladwell, M. (2005). *Blink: The power of thinking without thinking.* New York: Little, Brown and Company.

Goldberg, E. (2005). *The paradox of wisdom: How your mind can grow stronger as your brain grows older.* New York: Gotham Books.

Goleman, D. (2006). *Social intelligence: The new science of human relationships.* New York: Bantam.

Gopnik, A., Meltzoff, A., & Kuhl, P. (1999). *The scientist in the crib: Minds, brains, and how children learn.* New York: Morrow.

Gray, T. (1955). Elegy written in a country churchyard. In J. Bartlett (Ed.), *Bartlett's familiar quotations* (p. 348). Boston: Little, Brown and Company.

Hannaford, C. (2002). *Awakening the child within: A handbook for global parenting.* Captain Cook, HI: Jamilla Nur Publishing

Hawkins, J., & Blakeslee, S. (2004). *On intelligence: How a new understanding of the brain will lead to the creation of truly intelligent machines.* New York: Henry Holt.

Iacoboni, M. (2008). *Mirroring people. The new science of how we connect with others.* New York: Farrar, Straus, and Giroux.

Jensen, E. (2006). *Enriching the brain: How to maximize every learner's potential.* San Francisco: Jossey-Bass.

Johnson, S. (2005). *Everything bad is good for you: How today's popular culture is actually making us smarter.* New York: Riverhead Books.

Kagan, J. (1998). *Three seductive ideas.* Cambridge, MA: Harvard University Press.

Kagan, J., Herschkowitz, N., & Herschkowitz, E. (2005). *A young mind in a growing brain.* Mahwah, NJ: Lawrence Erlbaum Associates.

Klingberg, T. (2009). *The overflowing brain: Information overload and the limits of working memory.* New York: Oxford University Press.

Kluger, J., Walsh, B. Stein, J., Rawe, J. & Sayre, C. (2007, June 11). The science of appetite: Why we're hardwired to crave the wrong things, and what new research says we can do about it: A special health report. *Time Magazine, 169*(24), 48–82.

Kohn, A. (2005). *Unconditional parenting: Moving from rewards and punishments to love and reason.* New York: Atria.

LeDoux, J. (2002). *Synaptic self: How our brains become who we are.* New York: Viking.

Levitin, D. (2006). *This is your brain on music: The science of an obsession.* New York: Dutton.

Marcus, G. (2004). *The birth of the mind: How a tiny number of genes creates the complexities of human thought.* New York: Basic Books.

Meltzoff, A., & Prinz, W. (Eds.). (2002). *The imitative mind: Development, evolution, and brain bases.* Cambridge, UK: Cambridge University Press.

Morning sickness may be sign of a bright baby. (2009, May 07). *New Scientist.* Retrieved May 12, 2010, from http://www.newscientist .com/article/mg20227074.600-morning-sickness-may-be-sign-of-a-bright-baby.html.

Nash, J. (2007, January 29). The gift of mimicry. *Time Magazine, 169*(5), 108–113.

Neill, A. S. (1960). *Summerhill: A new view of childhood.* New York: St. Martin's Press.

Nesse, R., & Williams, G. (1994). *Why we get sick: The new science of Darwinian medicine.* New York: Random House.

Perkins, D. (1995). *Outsmarting I.Q.: The emerging science of learnable intelligence.* New York: Free Press.

Pinker, S. (2007). *The stuff of thought: Language as a window into human nature.* New York: Viking.

Posner, M., & Rothbart, M. (2007). *Educating the human Brain.* Washington, DC: American Psychological Association.

Prensky, M. (2009, February). H. Sapiens Digital: From digital immigrants and digital natives to digital wisdom. *Innovate: Journal of Online Education 5*(3). Retrieved May 6, 2010, from http://www .innovateonline.info/pdf/vol5_issue3/H._Sapiens_Digital-_From_Digital_Immigrants_and_Digital_Natives_to_Digital_Wisdom.pdf.

Profet, M. (1992). Pregnancy sickness as adaptation: A deterrent to maternal ingestion of teratogens. In J. Barkow (Ed.), *The adapted mind* (pp. 327–365). New York: Oxford University Press.

Provine, R. (2000). *Laughter: A scientific investigation.* New York: Viking.

Ramachandran, V. S. (2004). *A brief tour of human consciousness.* New York: PI Press.

Ramachandran, V. S. (2006). Mirror neurons and the brain in a vat. *Edge: The Third Culture.* Retrieved May 6, 2010, from http://www.edge.org/3rd_culture/ramachandran06/ramachandran06_index.html.

Ramachandran, V. S., & Oberman, L. M. (2006, November). Broken mirrors: A theory of autism. *Scientific American, 295*(5), 63–69.

Ratey, J. (with Hagerman, E.). (2008). *Spark: The revolutionary new science of exercise and the brain.* New York: Little, Brown and Company.

Restak, R. (2006). *The naked brain: How the emerging neurosociety is changing how we live, work, and love.* New York: Harmony Books.

Ridley, M. (2000). *Genome: The autobiography of a species in 23 chapters.* New York: Perennial.

Rizzolatti, G., Fogassi, L., & Gallese, V. (2006, November). Mirrors in the mind. *Scientific American, 295*(5), 54–62.

Rizzolatti, G., & Gallese, V. (2002). From mirror neurons to imitation: Facts and speculations. In A. Meltzoff & W. Prinz (Eds.), *The imitative mind: Development, evolution, and brain bases* (pp. 247–266). Cambridge, UK: Cambridge University Press.

Rizzolatti, G., & Sinigaglia, C. (2007). *Mirrors in the brain: How our minds share actions and emotions.* Oxford, UK: Oxford University Press.

Rousell, M. (2007). *Sudden influence: How spontaneous events shape our lives.* Westport, CT: Praeger.

Seuss, D. (1954). *Horton hears a Who!* New York: Random House.

Small, G., & Vorgan, G. (2008). *iBrain: Surviving the technological alteration of the human mind.* New York: Harper Collins.

Sousa, D. (2005). *How the brain learns* (3rd ed.). Thousand Oaks, CA: Corwin.

Sprenger, M. (2006). *Becoming a whiz at brain-based teaching* (2nd ed.). Thousand Oaks, CA: Corwin.

Stamm, J. (2007). *Bright from the start: The simple, science-backed way to nurture your child's developing mind from birth to three.* New York: Gotham.

Sternberg, R. (1985). *Beyond I.Q.: A triarchic theory of human intelligence.* New York: Cambridge University Press.

Sylwester, R. (2003). *A biological brain in a cultural classroom: Enhancing cognitive and social development through collaborative classroom management.* Thousand Oaks, CA: Corwin.

Sylwester, R. (2005). *How to explain a brain: An educator's handbook of brain terms and cognitive processes.* Thousand Oaks, CA: Corwin.

Sylwester, R. (2007). *The adolescent brain: Reaching for autonomy.* Thousand Oaks, CA: Corwin.

Taylor, S. (2002). *The tending instinct: How nurturing is essential to who we are and how we live.* New York: Times Books.

Wolf, P. (2010). *Brain matters: Translating research into classroom practice.* Alexandria, VA: Association for Supervision and Curriculum Development.

Wright, R. (2000). *Non-zero: The logic of human destiny.* New York: Pantheon.

ELECTRONIC RESOURCES

Information About the Brain

Eric Chudler's Neuroscience Resource Site. http://faculty .washington.edu/chudler/ehceduc.html

This is a very informative website with links to many other websites. See also Chudler's other website, *Neuroscience for Kids* (below).

The Charles A. Dana Foundation. http://www.dana.org

A broadly informative website suitable for both scientists and the general public, the website's *Brainy Kids Online* section is especially useful for educators.

Neuroguide.com. http://www.neuroguide.com

The Neuroguide is a comprehensive access to Internet websites on brain issues and to neuroscience information not easily found elsewhere. See especially *Best Bets.*

Neuroscience for Kids. http://faculty.washington.edu/chudler/ neurok.html

This website is a marvelous resource for information and exploratory projects for young people. See also Eric Chudler's Neuroscience Resource Site (above).

Public Broadcasting Service Teacher Source. http://www.pbs.org

PBS offers an excellent resource for educators on many topics, including the cognitive neurosciences. Type in *brain information* or *cognitive neuroscience* for useful information drawn from PBS programs.

The Washington University School of Medicine Neuroscience Tutorial. http://thalamus.wustl.edu/course

This website provides an excellent Internet tutorial on the brain and brain anatomy.

The World Wide Web Virtual Library: Neuroscience (Biosciences) http://neuro.med.cornell.edu/VL

This virtual library contains links to just about any website on brain and cognitive issues that one could imagine.

Whole Brain Atlas. http://www.med.harvard.edu/AANLIB/home.html

It's just what the title says—illustrations of anything you could possibly want to know about the human brain.

Practical Advice on Rearing and Teaching Children

American Academy of Child and Adolescent Psychiatry. http://www.aacap.org/cs/forFamilies

This website provides much credible, useful information on a wide variety of issues of concern to parents and educators, such as on popular culture and sexual abuse.

Child and Family Web Guide. http://www.cfw.tufts.edu/?/keyword/child-rearing/53/

Here you will find a comprehensive clearing house of recommended websites on a variety of issues related to parenting and educating children.

ERIC—Education Resources Information Center. http://www.eric.ed.gov/

This site is the world's largest digital library on a wide variety of educational issues and literature.

IAE-Pedia. Information Age Education (wiki) Pedia. http://IAE-pedia.org

On this website, you will find a wiki-type encyclopedia of useful information for parents and educators.

Keep Kids Healthy. http://www.keepkidshealthy.com

Practical advice and resources on health and safety can be found at this website offered by a pediatrician and support staff.

Librarians Internet Index. http://lii.org/

Here you will be able to access information on a wide variety of credible websites that contain useful information for educators and parents, such as on mass media/computers and children.

Raising Kids. http://www.lhj.com/relationships/family/raising-kids/

The website offers practical advice on issues related to child/adolescent parenting and teaching drawn from site consultants from the advice columns in the *Ladies' Home Journal*.

Health, Illness, and Disability

About.com. http://www.about.com/health/

Part of an extensive website (*about.com*) on many issues, *about.com/health* provides useful nontechnical information on a wide variety of illnesses and disabilities.

Association of Cancer Online Resources. http://www.acor.org/

The site provides access to a large number of online resources on cancer information and services.

Bright Futures. http://www.brightfutures.aap.org

This is the health and illness advice website of the American Academy of Pediatrics.

Centers for Disease Control. http://www.cdc.gov/vaccines/
Here, you will find the CDC website for information on vaccinations.

Cure Search. http://www.curesearch.org/
This website of two major children's cancer foundations offers useful information and resources.

Food and Nutrition Information Center. http://fnic.nal.usda.gov
This website, maintained by the U.S. Department of Agriculture, provides credible, accurate, and practical information and resources on nutrition.

Mayo Clinic. http://www.mayoclinic.com/
Here you will find a comprehensive guide to useful information on hundreds of illnesses.

National Center on Birth Defects and Developmental Disabilities. http://www.cdc.gov/ncbddd/index.html
This is a very informative outreach service of the U.S. Centers for Disease Control and Prevention.

Support for Families of Children With Disabilities. http://www.supportforfamilies.org/internetguide/index.html
Go to this website for an extensive listing and description of a wide variety of parent and educator Internet resources on children with disabilities.

Your Nutrition and Food Safety Resource. http://www.ific.org/nutrition/kids
This site is a very informative resource of the International Food Information Council. It covers all areas of concern for parents and educators.

Index

CORWIN

A SAGE Company

The Corwin logo—a raven striding across an open book—represents the union of courage and learning. Corwin is committed to improving education for all learners by publishing books and other professional development resources for those serving the field of PreK–12 education. By providing practical, hands-on materials, Corwin continues to carry out the promise of its motto: **"Helping Educators Do Their Work Better."**